Energy, Einstein, and the Great Depression

Bernard C. Beaudreau

Energy, Einstein, and the Great Depression

Macroeconomic Acceleration and Collapse

palgrave
macmillan

Bernard C. Beaudreau
Quebec City, QC, Canada

ISBN 978-3-032-26663-7 ISBN 978-3-032-26664-4 (eBook)
https://doi.org/10.1007/978-3-032-26664-4

This Palgrave Macmillan imprint is published by the registered company Springer Nature Switzerland AG, part of Springer Nature.
The registered company address is: Gewerbestrasse 11, 6330 Cham, Switzerland

If disposing of this product, please recycle the paper.

Preface

In an article published in Nash's *Pall Mall Magazine* in 1932 entitled *The Way to a New Prosperity*, 1921 Nobel Prize laureate in Physics Albert Einstein valiantly waded into the debate over the causes of the Great Depression, pointing to technical progress as the main culprit. Improvements in machinery, he argued, had reduced the demand for labor, thus reducing overall purchasing power, setting off a downward spiral. In his view, innovations that were intended to improve the human condition actually led to the worst economic downturn in history. Unable to identify just what inventions and/or innovations were driving record productivity growth, he nonetheless went on to argue that the solution lay in shortening the work week and raising wages.

This view was neither new nor novel, having been advanced by numerous other period writers, Rexford G. Tugwell, the Columbia University economics professor and architect of President Franklin D. Roosevelt's signature New Deal policy, the National Industrial Recovery Act, being one of the more influential. Businessmen and scholars alike waved an accusatory finger at technical progress. The problem, however, was one of definition—exactly what the technical progress was. Judging from the many accounts, it had to be significant, and it had to be such that all—or most—industries and sectors were affected.

It could be argued that the nondescript, amorphous nature of the alleged technical progress tainted, to the point of virtually invalidating, the resulting view of the events leading up to, and including, the Great Depression. In many regards, it was analogous to the Solow residual in contemporary growth theory, which is a nondescript, portmanteau-like residual measure of technical progress. Post-WWII technological innovation that gave the world the greatest period of sustained high growth is reduced to a single, nondescript residual variable. Put differently, it will come as little surprise to learn that if a scientist/scholar in whatever field is unable to identify "a" or "the" very cause of the phenomenon s/he is attempting to understand, then the rest of his/her analysis will fall on deaf ears. This is where this book fits in.

Drawing from recent findings on the role of acceleration in material processes of the 1920s and 1930s in the downturn (Beaudreau 2023), it provides the missing link so-to-speak, specifically an account of the technical progress that Einstein and his contemporaries overlooked and the technical progress that underlies his analysis—both diagnosis and prognosis. To this end, it begins by highlighting the existence of similar arguments made by period and later writers—in short, Einstein was not alone in pointing to improvements in technique throughout the 1920s. However, it extends the analysis by providing a detailed description of the "technical progress" referred to in each of his contributions as well as described in the majority of writings on productivity and output growth, namely, the electric unit drive–based acceleration of material processes throughout the 1920s, made possible by the emergence of large-scale public and private utilities providing low-cost power to companies. Its basic contribution lies in showing just how the widespread application of electric unit drive, by increasing the rated capacity of existing machinery and equipment throughout the US economy, ultimately led to the downturn.

This is achieved by invoking the basic underlying physics of electric unit drive–based acceleration in the US industry throughout the 1920s. Specifically, material processes are modeled using a combination of basic physics—classical mechanics, thermodynamics, and kinetics—and basic process engineering, allowing us to show how widespread electric unit drive–based acceleration increased the potential rated capacity of existing and new machinery and equipment thus increasing conventionally defined productivity. It avoids the arm-waving and nondescript nature of the technological unemployment literature.

Incorporated into a simple macroeconomic model, we are able to show that because companies were constrained on the demand side (i.e., by aggregate expenditure), they responded by reducing hours and employment—what Einstein referred to as technological unemployment. His prognosis, namely, a shorter work week and higher wages, is then reexamined from an ex post point of view, namely, in terms of what the post-1939 recovery actually looked like. In other words, can it be shown that his policy prescriptions were consistent with the conditions of the actual recovery?

The next chapter examines Einstein's later writings on institutions, notably on the market versus command economy debate—that is, the debate on individual incentives versus third party–based cooperation, economic justice, and social justice. While his writings about the underlying cause of the Great Depression (technical progress) were well received, notably by Yale University economics professor Irving Fisher, his later writings in the economic and social realm were the subject of much controversy, particularly his defense of government intervention. It will be shown that his ideas were not particularly revolutionary but rather were in keeping with period writings, some by leading scholars.

The last chapter entitled "The Structural Impediments to Incomizing Potential Output" examines the underlying problem from both a theoretical and policy point of view, providing historical references and proposed solutions. It is argued that had Einstein been aware of this century-old literature, his analysis would have been more convincing, if not more scholarly. They, however, should be seen as extremely laudable given that he was able to intuit a problem that was at the time a century old.

In short, the book shows why Einstein was right insofar as the causes of the Great Depression were concerned and a visionary insofar as the macroeconomic consequences of massive process-based technology shock in a capitalist, for-profit economy. This being said, it also points to an irony of sorts, namely, that despite his background in physics, specifically in the study of speed, acceleration, time, and space, he was unable to identify, to any significant degree, the inventions and innovations that lesser period writers pointed to. This is all the more surprising given that wealth creation (production) is a material process which, like all others, is powered by energy; then, it follows that any and all increases in wealth must invariably be energy-based as both labor and capital are not, according to classical mechanics, physically productive.

Hence, in addition to corroborating his diagnosis, the book goes further by outlining the physics behind the massive increase in the US's ability to produce wealth in the 1920s and 1930s, namely, a surge in electric power use that manifested itself in accelerated machine and process speeds throughout the economy. In this regard, it represents a first in the technological unemployment literature (Bix 2000) by providing a detailed account of the only possible form of technological innovation/technical progress that is consistent with the physical laws that govern material processes, namely, energy-based acceleration. In so doing, it provides a framework for understanding industrialization and the fallout from over two centuries of speed-ups.

Quebec City, QC, Canada

Bernard C. Beaudreau

Competing Interests The author has no competing interests to declare that are relevant to the content of this manuscript.

Contents

List of Figures

List of Tables

CHAPTER 1

Introduction

Abstract Throughout the Great Depression, a number of outsiders joined the debate over the causes, consequences, and possible solutions to the record unemployment and economic contraction. One such individual was the 1921 physics Nobel Prize laureate and greatest physicist of the twentieth century, Albert Einstein. In a series of magazine and newspaper articles, he pointed to technical progress as the cause of the downturn, outlining its effects on output and employment. This chapter provides a synopsis of his views, complete with the original articles. It also provides an outline of our attempt at rehabilitating his views in light of period evidence as well as recent advances in modeling material processes.

Keywords Great Depression • Outsiders • Albert Einstein • Technical progress

Throughout its 250-year history, the field of political economy has seen its share of outsiders chiming in on questions of heightened social and economic interest. In the nineteenth century, polymath Charles Babbage in 1832 penned *On the Economy of Machinery and Manufactures* in order to better understand the impact of the steam engine on productivity and output. In the twentieth century, 1921 Chemistry Nobel Prize laureate

B. C. Beaudreau, *Energy, Einstein, and the Great Depression*, https://doi.org/10.1007/978-3-032-26664-4_1

Frederick Soddy attempted to update production theory (i.e., neoclassical production theory) by invoking the laws of the physical world, specifically by incorporating basic physics in our understanding of wealth-generating material processes. A group of engineers at Columbia University known as the technocrats did likewise in the early 1930s, incorporating what they felt was the missing element, namely, energy.

In 1932, at what was the height of the Great Depression, Albert Einstein, the 1921 laureate of the Nobel Prize in physics threw his hat in the ring.[1] In an article entitled "The Way to a New Prosperity!," he pointed to technical progress as the chief cause of the downturn, which by then had become a full-blown depression (Table 1.1). By increasing productivity, it reduced the demand for labor, thus depressing purchasing power as overall wage income fell, setting off a downward spiral of income and expenditure. To counter this and restore prosperity, he advocated shortening the workweek and raising wages.

Other than his intellectual curiosity, what appeared to motivate his interest in the problem of the Great Depression was his view that something tragic had occurred, that something that was supposed to make society and the world better off by increasing wealth had gone horribly wrong.

Yale University economics professor Irving Fisher with whom Einstein corresponded with in the early 1930s held similar views insofar as technical progress was concerned (Fisher, 1930).

> *But after 1919, something happened. The implications of it are not sufficiently gauged. It was of enough significance to cause President Hoover's Committee on Recent Economic Changes to remark that "acceleration rather than structural change is the key to understanding our recent economic developments." The committee added: "But the breadth, scale and tempo of recent developments give them special importance." Fisher,* 1930, *p. 16*

He, however, disagreed with him insofar as the exact cause of the downturn, pointing to a phenomenon he referred to as debt deflation instead. That is, falling prices had the effect of transferring real wealth

[1] As mentioned earlier, Einstein's interest in the economic and political issues of the 1930s could be attributed to the time spent in post-WWI Germany when the Treaty of Versailles and its effects on the German economy were an integral part of the public discourse, as well as to the fallout for Germany of the Smoot-Hawley Tariff Act of 1930 which closed the US market to German exports, thus hindering its capacity to pay reparations (see Rowe & Schulmann, 2009).

Table 1.1 Einstein's description of technical progress

Definition	*Source*
Rapid progress of production methods	"The way to a new prosperity!" By Albert Einstein Nash's *Pall Mall*, 1932
Technical progress	Ibid
The improvement in the apparatus of production through technical invention and organization	"World ills laid to machines" By Einstein in Berlin speech Special cable to the New York times
Industrial technique	Ibid
Improvement of the mechanical apparatus and the organization	"Letter to Irving fisher"

from borrowers to savers. Einstein disagreed, pointing to insufficient purchasing power, owing to insufficient buying power due to low wages and technological unemployment. Fisher dismissed the latter view on the grounds that the new techniques in question had resulted in higher wages.

In time, the novelty and celebrity factor would peter out, and Einstein's forays in the debate over the Great Depression would fall into obscurity. However, the very issues he raised would resurface in the Roosevelt Administration's 1933 National Industrial Recovery Act which, like Einstein, attributed to the downturn to technological change and insufficient purchasing power. To remedy the situation, it called for across-the-board wage increases and public spending.

This book sets out to show just why Einstein was right and why the period literature on technological progress as the cause of the Great Depression fell into obscurity. In short, it is argued that the main problem, then as now, was the failure on the part of its many proponents to clearly identify the "technical progress" or technological shock in question.[2] Writers like Irving Fisher pointed to a panoply of possible causes without, however, showing exactly how they contributed to what President Hoover's Committee on Recent Economic Changes referred to as

[2] This is also the chief criticism leveled against the real business cycle (RBC) literature, namely, the inability to identify positive and negative productivity shocks.

"acceleration" and "tempo."[3] Einstein was also guilty of this, as in none of his writings or talks was he able to put a finger on (or relativize) the exact cause.

In short, it is shown that by incorporating basic physics into a simple model of material processes (production functions), the key element in the technological progress in the 1920s can be identified and incorporated in a macroeconomic model of the Great Depression. Specifically, it is shown that the rapid spread of electric unit drive in the 1910s, but especially in the 1920s, increased operating speeds of virtually all material processes, thus increasing productivity. By increasing energy consumption per unit of capital, material processes were sped up, thus increasing conventionally defined productivity.

The irony of it all, however, is the fact that this (i.e., increased overall energy consumption) was lost on the world's greatest physicist, someone for whom energy in its many forms was at the center of his seminal contributions. Thus, in many regards, Frederick Soddy, who won the 1921 Nobel Prize in Chemistry and who was also interested in economic growth in the 1920s, had explicitly incorporated energy into his ambitious reformulation of basic economics (i.e., Cartesian Economics 1924) around the laws of physics. In many ways, so too had a group of Columbia University engineering professors known as the technocrats who proposed a science-based approach to understanding wealth focused on energy.

On a broader level, this book is in keeping with the view that while macroeconomic modeling (i.e., DSGE models) is a worthwhile endeavor, progress in the field can only be achieved by first understanding epoch-defining events such as the Great Depression and the Financial Meltdown of 2008. Then and only then can and should attempts be made to develop more general, all-encompassing frameworks.

Appendix 1: Einstein's Writings on Technological Progress and the Great Depression

Nash's Pall Mall *1932 Article*

The Way to a New Prosperity!
By Albert Einstein
Nash's Pall Mall, 1932.

[3] If nothing else, both of these words or expressions connote speed and acceleration.

The one thing that can encourage anyone outside the field of economics to voice an opinion on the nature of the present economic difficulties is the hopeless confusion of opinions among experts.
What I have to say isn't new and doesn't represent more than the conviction of an independent and honest person, unhampered by national and class prejudices—of a person who wishes nothing more that the well-being of all mankind and the most harmonious formation of human life
This conviction of mine is that our present crisis does not have the character of former crises in as much as it is founded upon an entirely new condition, one resulting from the rapid progress of production-methods—only a fraction of the human working-power at our disposal is now necessary to produce the world's total demand for the necessities of life. The inevitable result of this is that only part of our human working-power can find utilization, in view of to-day's state of working methods. While one portion of our working-power is being unreasonably claimed—perhaps overworked—the remainder is automatically cast entirely out of the production process—left idle.
The demand for products, and thereby the profitableness of production naturally sinks under such conditions. Enterprises become bankrupt, further increased unemployment, then follows, swells the loss of confidence in enterprises; then comes the insolvency of banks resulting from the sudden withdrawal of deposits, and finally complete stagnation arrives.
I have also sought to trace back the present crisis to its other causes with which I shall now deal.
In the matter of over-production it is necessary to distinguish between two things: real over-production and apparent over-production. Real over-production I understand as production which is so high that it exceeds demand. This may be present apply in the United States as regards automobiles and wheat, although even this is doubtful.
Generally speaking, over-production signifies production of one kind of merchandise in greater quantity than can be sold under prevailing circumstances, despite the scarcity of such merchandise among consumers. I call this "apparent" over-production. In this case, it is not the demand that is lacking, but the buying power of the consumer. Such apparent over-production is only another expression of the present crisis and cannot, therefore, be used as an explanation for it. If one holds over-production responsible for the present crisis, one operating only with delusory causes.
Again, obligations to pay reparations are burdening debtor nations and their economies are forcing them to export-dumping, thereby damaging in turn the creditor nations; this cannot be denied. But the appearance of the crisis in the United States (which is protected by high tariff walls) shows that this cannot be the main cause of our world crisis.

Again, shortage of money in debtor nations caused by reparations at very best can be used as an argument for the suspension of these payments, but certainly not as an explanation for the world crisis.

Furthermore, the erection of many new tariff walls; the increase of unproductive armament burdens; political insecurity because of the potential danger of war—all these make Europe's situation much worse, without materially affecting America. The appearance of the crisis in America also shows therefore, that these cannot be the most important cause of the crisis, either.

Once more, the loss of Chinese and Russian markets caused a damage to world economy that cannot possibly make itself felt strongly in America either, and therefore cannot be the main cause of the crisis.

In the other hand, for me it has become an established fact that the technical progress which, in itself, would be destined to relieve humanity of a large part of the burden of work necessary for its maintenance is the chief cause of our present plight. Therefore, many critics who agree with me, seriously want to prohibit the introduction of more and more mechanical improvements. This is obviously nonsense. But, how can a more sensible way out of this dilemma be found?

If in one way or another one should succeed in preventing the buying power of the masses from sinking below a certain minimum-point, measured in merchandise value, such stagnations of economic circulation as we are presently experiencing would be made impossible.

Logically the simplest but also the riskiest method for attaining this condition is a complete fixed plan or method: the production and distribution of the necessities of life by means of the community. This is materially what to-day is being tried in Russia, and much in the future will depend upon what results will mature from this tremendous experiment.

To expound prophecies along this line would, however, be presumptuous.

Does such a system, for instance, permit production equally as efficient as that which allows the initiative of the individual more liberty?

Again, can this system be maintained at al without the reign of terror that has been maintained up to this time and to which not one of us, oriented "westwardly" would wish to expose himself?

Doesn't such a rigid centralized economic system, too, lean towards protectionism and isolation as against advantageous innovations?

One must consider these things but one must care not to allow such doubts to become prejudices which might prevent the formation of objective judgement.

I personally believe that the whole of these methods are to be preferred which respect traditions and customs to the utmost possible degree compatible with the aim in view. I also believe that any rapid change to public ownership is disadvantageous in the interest of the production of goods; private initiative should be allowed its field of activity, except in so far as it hasn't already been cast aside by economy as the result of cartelization.

In all cases restriction of free unhampered economy is necessary in two respects: the working week in all individual branches must be shortened law, so unemployment will be abolished systematically, and in fixing minimum wages, care must be taken that the buying power of workers corresponds to production.
Furthermore, the price-fixing of these branches of production which have attained a monopolistic character through the organization of the producers should be controlled by the state to the extent of keeping capital accumulation withing a reasonable limit and preventing any artificial restriction of production and consumption.
In this way, it would probably be possible to establish an equilibrium between production and consumption without too great a restriction of free initiative and at the same time eliminate the disproportionate superiority of the owners of the means of production machinery over wage earners (in the widest sense).

Prof. Einstein's Recipe for a New Prosperity

Prof. Einstein says:
The world depression is not caused by
1.Production exceeding the demand, or
2. Debtor nations, burdened with reparations payments, dumping exports on creditor nations, or
3. The loss of Chinese and Russian markets.
But by machinery
Destined to relieve the world of some of the work necessary for its maintenance.
The Cure lies in
Preventing the buying power of the masses sinking below a certain minimum point measured in merchandise value.
This can be done by
1.Community control of supply and demand but this must be managed so as to allow individual freedom for his initiative and avoid rapid change from private to public ownership, since this would be disadvantageous to production,
2. Shortening the working week to eliminate unemployment,
3.Fixing the minimum wage so that the worker's buying power will correspond to production.
This will result in
Striking a balance between production and consumption without too much restriction of initiative and eliminating the disproportionate superiority of owners of the means of production over the workers.

Letter to Irving Fisher

Albert Einstein's Letter to Irving Fisher. Sources: Irving Fisher Papers (Yale University) and Albert Einstein Papers (Hebrew University). Underlines in the Original
10 *February* 1933

Very dear Mr. Fisher,
Thank you for your enlightening book, which I have read with great interest. I assume that the criticism of my little speech was with regard the statement that the main cause of today's situation were the improvement of the mechanical apparatus and the organization. Based upon your careful studies, you state that this crisis is caused, just as the previous ones, primarily by over-indebtedness. This seems to be very convincing. Only I think that over-indebtedness itself cannot be considered the prima causa[4]*. Unfortunately, it is hard to see which is cause and which is effect.*
Among your suggestions, I like the suggestion best, where you want to stabilize the Index by abandoning the gold standard. This has long since been one of my favorite ideas. If this has been done in time, certainly the present collapse would have been less serious. As long as these high tariffs exist, however, this plan would be hard to realize internationally.
I disagree with you, however, on one point: that you compare the present situation equal to previous crises. Now, as before, I am convinced that we are facing a new situation: a fraction of previous working hours suffices to produce today all consumer goods that are desirable and necessary for all. Therefore, I am firmly convinced that without legal compensatory measures, the economy will not be able to use all available manpower and thus produce a fairly even purchasing power of the public[5]*. Without special control a devaluation of the actual labor force will ensue. Thus, a completely undesirable chronic shrinking of the consumption, and thus of the production, will necessarily follow. This seems to me the point where today's economic system must fail when the otherwise relatively well functioning apparatus of a free economy falters. I don't think, as many liberal theoretical thinkers do, that creating new, superfluous branches of industry will automatically correct the evil.*
I do not maintain that an excessive supply of labor is virtually something new. But previously this was based on the poor distribution of the soil and other abuses, but not on fundamental conditions of the economy.

Respectfully yours,
Einstein

[4] Fisher translated instead as "legal stabilization control."
[5] Fisher translated instead as "equal buying power of the consumers."

Appendix 2: Newspaper Articles

World Ills Laid to Machines
By Einstein in Berlin Speech
Special Cable to The New York Times.

BERLIN, Oct. 21.—Discussing the effects of natural science on man's life, Professor Albert Einstein in a lecture tonight deplored the fact that the industrial technique which was meant to serve the world's progress by liberating mankind from the slavery of labor was now about to overwhelm its creators.
He characterized the great distress of the present times as the result of domination by man-made machines, but blamed technique not as much as lack of organization in economic and social life, the stabilization of which is one of the chief tasks of the present time.
Regarding the direct effects of natural science upon life, Professor Einstein stressed the philosophic theory of determinism, which he said was almost generally recognized today.
The New York Times
Published: October 22, 1931

EINSTEIN TRACES SLUMP TO MACHINE
Improved Methods of Production Eliminate Labor and Buying Power, He Says.
WAR DEBTS SECONDARY
Understanding of Depression Will Ease World Friction, He Tells Pasadena Audience.
GREED AND FEAR BLAMED
H. M. Robinson Urges Freeing Economic Machinery—Dr. W. B. Munro for Cooperation of Nations.
Special to The New York Times.
PASADENA, Calif., Jan. 23.—Declaring that the world-wide depression was not caused by the war debt situation but by new machinery and more efficient industrial organization which had brought about the displacement of labor and lowered purchasing power, Dr. Albert Einstein delivered an address in English here tonight in a symposium on "American and the World Situation."
The depression is understood to have been caused by economic evolution instead of by the war debt problem, the most dangerous threat to world peace will vanish, Dr. Einstein declared.
The recognition of the fact that all nations are facing a single major problem, he added, should lessen the distrust of nations which engender predatory action, give greater prominence to sympathy and spiritual force, and lead to spiritual forces as the principal hopes for overcoming the crisis.

Thousands Pack Auditorium.
Several thousand persons were gathered at the Civic Auditorium to hear the address. Besides Dr. Einstein, those who spoke were Henry M. Robinson, Los Angeles banker and member of the Dawes Reparations Commission, and Dr. William B. Munro, historian and political scientist and member of the executive council of the California Institute of Technology. The symposium was conducted under the auspices of the Southern California League of Nations Association.
Only by the dissipation of international distrust, he said, can existing evils be overcome, since the present economic antagonism is an extension of the international crisis in economic life, Dr. Einstein said.
"The improvement in the apparatus of production through technical invention and organization has decreased the need for human labor," he said. "And thereby has caused the elimination of a part of labor from the economic life and the progressive decrease in the purchasing power of the consumers.
"As the war debts, any nation, as the final analysis, can pay only through the sale of its products to other nations. War debts must be paid down to an amount equal to the value of goods the creditor nation is willing to buy from the debtor nation. In other words, the United States cannot expect France to pay back more than the value of the goods France can dispose of in America."
Aside from the problem of war debts, he said, the technical and economic problems, as third. War debts probably must be revised in order to restore balance.
Dr. Munro Urges Budget Action.
Dr. Munro declared that the most fundamental issue that confronts the world today is "the momentous question whether two great continents, America and Europe, can cooperate in a supreme effort to preserve the institutions of free government from collapse."
"The steadying influence that in world depression like the present we can so far see when there are the war debts situation and so long as the two continents remain apart."
"The war debts situation and world depression are closely related."
All nations are in it, he declared.
Dr. Munro urged the adjournment of politics and the display by Congress of half the good sense, patience, thrift and resourcefulness which the business men of our country are showing in this crisis.
The most important need from Congress, he said, is a balanced national budget. A balanced national budget would do more to revive the drooping spirits of American business than any or all of the bizarre plans which are now being dangled in the halls of national legislation.
The New York Times
Published: January 24, 1933
Copyright © The New York Times

References

Fisher, I. (1930). *The stock market crash–and after*. The Macmillan Company.

Rowe, D. E., & Schulmann, R. (Eds.). (2009). *Einstein on politics: His private thoughts and public stands on nationalism, Zionism, war, peace, and the bomb*. Princeton University Press.

CHAPTER 2

Technical Progress and the Great Depression: Literature Review

Abstract This chapter examines technical progress in the United States in the pre-Great Depression era. It is argued that because of the underdeveloped nature of production theory at the time, many of the key developments were either overlooked or misunderstood by period writers. It is shown that foremost among these developments was the introduction of a new power drive technology known as electric unit drive that resulted in greater operating speeds and greater productivity throughout the economy.

Keywords Technical progress • Roaring Twenties • Electric unit drive • Acceleration

Introduction

This chapter focuses on technical progress in the pre-Great Depression era—that is, the period that Einstein was particularly interested in. It is argued that because of the underdeveloped nature of production theory at the time, many of the innovations were overlooked and/or misunderstood, not unlike growth theory today, where technological change is formalized in terms of a catch-all, portmanteau-style variable, the Solow

B. C. Beaudreau, *Energy, Einstein, and the Great Depression*,
https://doi.org/10.1007/978-3-032-26664-4_2

residual (total factor productivity). The discussion includes contributions in two time periods, namely, the pre-Great Depression era and the post-Great Depression—that is, ex-post descriptions of what Einstein referred to as "technical progress."

Productivity Growth in the 1920s (the Roaring Twenties)

Today, a century after the fact, the Roaring Twenties remain somewhat of an enigma, productivity-wise. After all, output and productivity exploded, yet the cause or causes remain shrouded in mystery. Referring to Table 2.1 which presents a non-exhaustive list of the various causes, both period (i.e., contemporary) and subsequent, three factors stand out, namely, the introduction of a new power source in the form of electric power, the mechanization of many material processes (i.e., production lines) and organizational (of production) innovations, and the latter being largely the result of the former as companies reorganized factory layouts.

As shown, the majority of the writers pointed to electric power as the key innovation, without, however, being able to make the link between it and productivity. A good example is Irving Fisher who, in his defense of the stock market boom, pointed to the increase in purchased electrical power (see Fig. 2.1), which he used as a proxy for the ongoing conversion to electric unit drive. This is consistent with Warren Devine (1983), who pointed out that throughout this period, electric wires were replacing gearing, belting, and shafting in manufacturing, but that the ultimate prime mover continued to be fossil fuels, hydro, and wind.[1] Just how and why this would lead to greater productivity is not clear. Some pointed to the resulting improved factory designs, while others pointed to improved flow through. Still, others pointed to the resulting automation.[2]

While not referring to electric unit drive per se, Harvard Business School business historian Alfred D. Chandler (1977) was one of the first to invoke greater process speed as the principal cause of greater productivity. As he put it, "In modern mass production, as in modern

[1] Electricity as such is not a prime mover, but rather a transmission technology. Throughout this period, dynamos, wires, and individual electric motors were replacing the cumbersome gearing, belting, and shafting of the nineteenth century.

[2] These changes were not confined to the United States but had spread to European countries, especially Germany and Great Britain (see Beaudreau, 1996, p. 126).

Table 2.1 The causes of the Roaring Twenties: period and contemporary views

Author	*Cause*
Period works	
Filene (1923)	Mass production
Ford (1926a)	Mass production, electric power, speed, and accuracy
Foster and Catchings (1927)	Our greatly increased productive capacity
Tugwell (1927)	Electric power
Tryon (1927)	New power sources
Thomas (1928)	Large-scale production
Report of the Committee on Recent Economic Changes of the President's Conference on Unemployment (1929)	Acceleration of existing plant and equipment
Fisher (1930)	Purchased electric power, new products, and improved management
Brookings (1932)	Mass production[a]
Scott et al. (1933)	Increasing use of power
Polakov (1933)	Power production, the new power age
Chase (1934)	The new technique of mass production
Bohn and Ely (1935)	Production and transmission of electricity for light and power
Soule (1947)	Electric unit drive
Giedion (1948)	Automation (e.g., bread production in the 1920s)
Recent works	
Lorant (1967)	Technological change (ex., chemical industry, Weizmann fermentation process)
Chandler (1977)	Process speed, increased throughput rates
Devine (1983)	Electric power, increased flow of production as a result of plant layout
Cohen (1984)	Increasingly sophisticated use of electric power in pulp and paper manufacturing processes
Oshima (1984)	Increase in the price of unskilled labor leading to mechanization
Wright (1990)	Increased utilization of America's endowment of natural resources
Field (2003)	Greater total factor productivity (TFP)

[a]It is important to note that mass production was first and foremost acceleration-based. Henry Ford, the proverbial father of modern mass production, defined it as "the focusing on a manufacturing project speed of the principles of power, accuracy, economy, system continuity and accuracy and speed (Ford, 1926b, p. 821)." It turns out that all of these attributes are speed-based. It is also important to point out that the assembly line was not a novel concept. What was novel was the speed at which everything in the plant moved

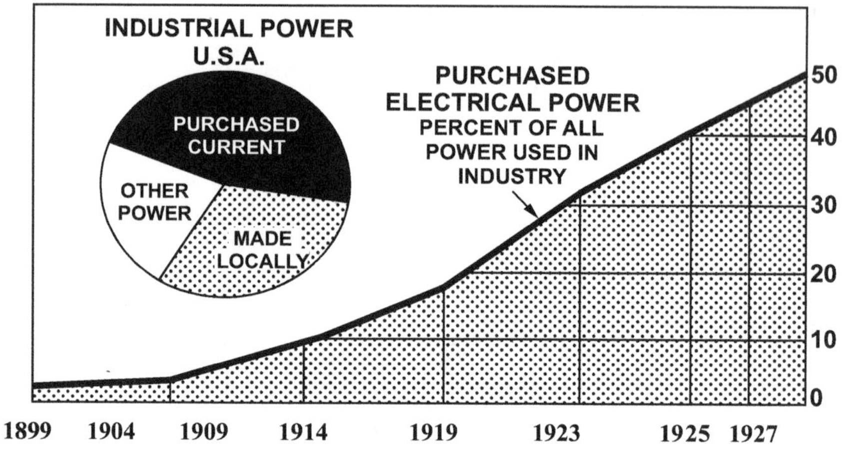

Fig. 2.1 Irving Fisher: purchased electrical power and electric unit drive

mass distribution and modern transportation and communications, economies resulted more from speed than from size. It was not the size of the manufacturing establishment in terms of the number of workers and the amount and value of productive equipment, but the velocity of throughput and the resulting increase in volume that permitted economies that lowered costs and increased output per worker and machine" (Chandler, 1977, p. 244). Walter Polakov (1933) referred to something he called the rate of production, which can be understood as a reference to acceleration and speed. Specifically, output was an increasing function of time, the number of employees, and the rate of production.[3]

What is abundantly clear, judging from these contributions, is the growing need to incorporate energy into the core of economic analysis, specifically in production theory. However, as is often the case, the devil was in the details. How could this be done? By simply appending a new variable $E(t)$ to the standard neoclassical production function? Accordingly, an increase in energy, ceteris paribus, will increase output. But how and why? What form of energy? And just how does energy enter production? The answer, according to many observers, was through kinetics or movement—that is, through machine speed. Greater energy consumption resulted in

[3]Output = $T \times E \times R$, where T = time, E = employees, and R = rate of production or machine speed.

greater machine speeds and hence greater output per unit of time, a fact made abundantly clear by Henry Ford in his description of mass production.

> *Mass production is not merely quantity production for this may be had with none of the requisites of mass production. Nor is it merely machine production, which also may exist without a resemblance to mass production. Mass production is the focusing upon a manufacturing project of the principles of power, accuracy, economy, system, continuity and speed.* (Ford, 1926b, *p. 821)*

The General Electric Company, one of the chief architects of the electric-unit-drive revolution, pointed to increased machine speed—controlled machine speed—as one of the defining features of modernity and of productivity growth. Under the title of *Today is the Day of Speed*, it maintained that

> *Our transportation systems, our industrial processes, our factory machinery—all these have felt the magic hand of speed,—controlled speed that has given us more things to enjoy and more time in which to enjoy them; that has produced more goods for more people at less cost and that has created a better standard of living for the average man. These are the benefits of ever-increasing speed and accurate control.*

Graham Laing, in "Towards Technocracy," pointed to machine speed as a key factor in the unprecedented productivity gains in the 1920s and 1930s.

> *Industrial processes have been speeded up, new inventions are being added to manufacturing, new economies of personnel and of management have been made in industry. The 1929 production can undoubtedly be achieved with thousands, and probably millions, fewer workers.* (Laing, 1933, *p. 23)*

Alfred Chandler, in his classic work on early twentieth-century US business organizations, echoed this view, generalizing it to the US economy as a whole.

> *In modern mass production, as in modern mass distribution and modern transportation and communications, economies resulted more from speed than from size. It was not the size of the manufacturing establishment in terms of the number of workers and the amount and value of productive equipment, but the velocity of throughput and the resulting increase in volume that permitted*

> *economies that lowered costs and increased output per worker and per machine.* (Chandler, 1977, *p. 244)*

Sidney Sonenblum, in his extensive work on electrification and productivity growth in manufacturing, also pointed to speed, specifically the acceleration of the rate of throughput, as a key element in productivity growth:

> *During these years, the focus of managerial attention shifted from enlarging the scale of operations to increasing operating efficiency by speeding up the rate of throughput in the plant. High priority was assigned to modifications of factory design and layout in order to better integrate worker and machine tasks. Advances in the electrification of machine drive were indispensable to the realization of these new objectives and may, indeed, have served to stimulate the new managerial perspectives that emerged.* (Sonenblum, 1990, *p. 291)*

Running through each of these accounts of speed and its role in productivity is the notion of control. The General Electric Company referred to "accurate control," while Ford referred to "accuracy, system and continuity." Hence, speed and control are to be understood as complementary inputs. Theoretically, control can be defined in terms of four functions: (*i*) constancy of speed, (*ii*) minimal breakdown-related downtime, (*iii*) sub-process coordination, and (*iv*) machine programming. Put differently, the better able is the firm/engineer at maintaining a constant speed, the greater the output. The same holds for machine breakdown. As not all machines/sub-processes operate at the same speed, it is essential—in order to avoid bottlenecks—to coordinate speeds throughout the plant. Lastly, because firms typically produce many different goods/models of goods with the same machinery, it stands to reason that more efficient machine programming will reduce downtime and, hence, increase the average operating speed per period of time.

According to Warren T. Devine (1990), control technologies underwent a series of innovations in the twentieth century that were instrumental in increasing machine speed. In a nutshell, hydraulic drive and control mechanisms gave way to servomechanisms, which in the 1950s gave way to numerical control, which reduced machine downtime considerably. Not only would productivity rise as a result of greater machine speeds (i.e., owing to greater energy use), but the machines themselves would be more fully utilized in any given time period. He noted

Numerically-controlled machinery had a number of advantages over conventional manually controlled machinery. The time required to get a newly designed part into production—the machine setup time—was sometimes as much as 65 to 75 percent less with numerical control. (Devine, 1990, *p. 50)*

Evidence from the Popular Press

While it could be argued that the state of production theory in the post-WWI period acted as an impediment to the economics profession in identifying and analyzing the effects of the new power drive technology on productivity and output for economists, such was not the case for journalists in the popular press who followed with great interest the changes brought about by the new power-drive technology.

The following excerpts from period newspapers from across the country are examples of the many reports of electric unit drive found throughout the 1920s.[4] The first, taken from the *Berkeley Daily Gazette*, highlights the important role played by electric unit drive in a number of industries. However, it also mentions that 125,000 industrial establishments have yet to convert, highlighting the immense potential that would be released in the event that they did so. The next, from *Devils Lake World and Inter Ocean*, describes in detail the advantages of electric unit drive, both cost-wise and speed-wise. It opens with a metaphor involving squeezing lemons, pointing to the efficiency and speed of the electrical squeezer. The third is an example of an industry (i.e., cotton mills) that converted from steam engine–driven belting, gearing, and shafting to electric unit drive, again providing a glimpse of the enormous impact of electric unit drive on machine speeds and efficiency. The fourth, taken from the *Great Falls Tribune*, describes in detail the impact of electric unit drive on paper making.

Berkeley Daily Gazette, October 19, 1920, p.9, Berkeley, California.
MANY INDUSTRIES AIDED BY ELECTRICAL DRIVE
Information compiled by the General Electric company has just been issued showing what the electric unit drive has done for the chemical industry.
The government nitrate plant at Muscle Shoals has the largest installation in the world of synchronous motors driving air compressors, this statement shows. In other phases of the chemical industry, such as ball mills which reduce ore to powder, ammonia and carbon dioxide refrigerating machinery, and centrifu-

[4] These articles are among hundreds that were consulted and are included for their representative nature.

gal, rotary and plunger pumps, the efficient electric motor has come into its own so completely that the modern chemist, according to the announcement of the General Electric company, depends continually upon this electrical product.
Stories of increased production due to electric drive have come out of a number of industries of late, matching this declaration of increased production in chemical plants through this means. All this is the reason for plans now maturing by electrical manufacturers for displaying industrial electric equipment at most of the large electrical shows of the fall. It is estimated that more than 125,000 industrial establishments in the United States are as yet not electrically equipped or operated. This is true, too, despite the fact that a year ago over five million electric motors were in use throughout the country.
BIG INCREASE IN ELECTRICAL INDUSTRY SHOWN
The continuing activity and prosperity of the electrical industry is evidenced by the volume of business reported by the Western Electric company whose sales are running at a higher rate than at any other period in the company's history. For eight months of the current year its domestic billings showed a total volume of $119,500,000 indicating domestic sales for the year of approximately $190,000,000. This does not include its export business from America nor sales of its foreign affiliated companies. The export and foreign business will probably reach a volume of $38,000,000, bringing the total business up to more than $225,000,000 for the year. The domestic sales will exceed the 1919 business by over $60,000,000 and are greatly in excess of the company's largest previous year, 1917, when domestic billings amounted to $142,000,000. This is especially worthy of note when it is considered that in 1917 the sales were materially affected by the heavy buying of the United States government, while in the present year the business is in all lines of the company's activities and in all sections of the county. This is true not only with respect to telephone apparatus but is especially marked in such labor saving devices as washing machines, sewing machines, vacuum cleaners and also in farm power and light plants.
Devils Lake World and Inter Ocean, August 10, 1916, p. 4
SAVING DOLLARS WITH ELECTRICITY
An electric lemon squeezer will extract the juice from a lemon in five seconds by the watch. It is estimated that one cent will pay for electricity enough to squeeze 720 lemons. Several foundries compared the cost of making their own electricity and buying it from a central station. They found a total average saving of 1.32 cents per horse power in favor of central station power.
A punch bowl which will cool a gallon of punch and keep it ice cold for three hours without the addition of ice is made by an electric refrigerating plant in sunny Georgia. The bowl is made of solid ice frozen in an iron form. The electric "shoeing" machine now has an extensive use in many car repair shops. It is a machine which goes under a car, lifts up the trucks one at a time and grinds the

noisy flat spots off of the wheels without removing the car trucks—for merely an expensive and tedious process.

A saving of from 40 to 50 per cent in the amount of energy necessary to run a steel rolling mill is effected with the electric drive, according to an engineering paper read before a meeting of engineers in Pennsylvania. Tests demonstrated that ingots could be rolled in from 2 to 16 seconds less with the electric drive than with the steam drive.

Electricity saves the owners of the great lake steamer Cicoa $500 every time the boat is loaded and unloaded. The steamer carries 4,000,000 pounds of pig iron and with it her own lifting magnet as a substitute for longshoremen. Electricity energizes the coils of the lifting magnet when it is lowered into the hold and causes the pigs of iron to stick to the magnet. When it is hoisted out of the depths of the ship a ton of pig iron comes with it. Cutting off the current releases the load of iron and drops it in cars or on the wharf. It costs but $100 to unload or load the vessel, a task which it would cost $600 to perform with a crew of longshoremen.

Dubuque Telegraph Herald, October 3, 1921, Pg. 7

ELECTRICITY IN INDUSTRY

The modern factory is a network of electrically driven machinery. From the incoming switchboard to the last motor in the remotest corner, electricity transmits its silent, powerful energy to every part of the plant.

In the making of a phonograph, for instance, electricity plays a most important part. From the cutting of the original record to the final polishing of the cabinet, electric motors drive the machinery that shapes, forms and finishes each separate piece.

The rough lumber is sawed, planed, and sanded by electrically driven machines. The intricate parts of the motor mechanism are turned, drilled and polished by electrically driven lathes and tools. The delicate mechanism itself is assembled and tested with the aid of electric power.

And when the instrument is finally completed, it is an electric motor that drives the turntable and reproduces the music that has been recorded.

The Dubuque Electric Company is prepared to supply electric power for all industrial purposes. Our rates are low, our service is reliable, and our territory is unsurpassed for industrial opportunities. Let us show you what electricity can do for your business.

Gainesville News, February 20, 1918, Pg. 1

GAINESVILLE'S TWO BIG MILLS INSTALLING ELECTRIC DRIVE

One of Largest Electrical Contracts Ever Signed in South; Makes Gainesville "The Electric City"

Work on the installation of electric drive in Gainesville's two large cotton mills, the Pacolet at New Holland and Gainesville Mill near the Southern depot, is well under way. This work was begun some weeks since, when material began *arriving to fill the contract. The contract for this change from steam to electricity was secured by Mr. Sam H. Browne, local manager of the Georgia Railway & Power Co., on May 18, 1917, and was one of the largest contracts for electric power ever signed in the South. Some conception of its magnitude is apparent when the fact is considered that the change will involve an initial expenditure upon the part of the power company and mill people of over $200,000.00.*

The inside wiring and motors are being installed by Huntington & Guerry, electrical contractors of Greenville, S. C. More than five hundred motors, ranging in size from 5 to 150 horse power, will be necessary to equip the two mills with the electric drive, 300 at Pacolet and about 225 at Gainesville Mill. The power company now has several crews at work on the change, and rapid progress is being made. One crew is installing the twelve big transformers recently received. Four of these will go to the Dunlap plant, four to Pacolet and four to Gainesville mill. The company has constructed a pole line and a crew is now at work stringing wires for the 38,000 volt transmission line from the Dunlap plant to the mills. About 6,000 horse-power will be furnished for the operation of the mills.

The Pacolet mill was built in 1900, and began operations in 1901. The cost of its construction was approximately $1,000,000. It is a five-story structure. The Gainesville mill was constructed and began operations at about the same time. It cost about $500,000 and is also a five-story structure.

The two mills have in operation 100,000 spindles, the Pacolet 57,000 and Gainesville Mills 43,000. They have consumed annually about 35,000 bales of cotton, or about three times the crop of Hall county. Both mills are located on the main line of the Southern railway, and have mill villages. The Pacolet has about 650 operatives, and the Gainesville mill 350.

Great Falls Tribune, May 15, 1921, p. 30

THE NEW SPEED MAKER

General Electric Sectional Drive: New Drive Makes High Speed

Now the biggest paper machines can produce paper at a thousand feet a minute, and a machine is under construction which is expected to run at 1200 feet a minute. Paper mill men everywhere become absorbed in this result, wholly revolutionary in their trade, and in the means by which it was accomplished—the sectionalized electric drive developed and perfected by the General Electric company.

The first experiments with a sectionalized drive—which is a mode of drive by which each section of the machine has its own individual motor, direct-connected—were made about twelve years ago. Engineers of the General Electric company performed tests in a paper mill in Maine, and there worked out the principle of the ideal drive now in actual use.

The sectional drive makes it possible to secure any speed desired for each section, and to maintain that speed with absolute accuracy regardless of load varia-

tions. It eliminates the long line shafts and complicated gearing that were formerly necessary, and reduces the power required to drive the machine.
The result is that paper can be produced at speeds that were formerly impossible, and with a quality that could not be obtained with the old methods. The sectional drive has made possible the tremendous increase in paper production that has taken place in recent years, and has helped to make possible the low prices at which paper is now sold.

A number of things stand out. First is the breadth of the electric-unit-drive revolution, so to speak. The conversion to electric unit drive was not restricted to manufacturing, but rather affected virtually all industries, going as far as multiplying many times over the productivity of a lemon squeezer. Second is the fact that all refer to the greater efficiency that electric unit drive–based acceleration produced. Last is the geographic breadth of the electric unit drive. From Gainesville, South Carolina; to Berkeley, California; to Grand Falls, Montana; to Dubuque, Iowa, electric unit drive was vastly increasing America's ability to produce wealth.

In the next section, the changes described here are formalized in terms of a theoretically consistent and empirically consistent model of output. By theoretically consilient, it should be understood as the property of being consistent or in keeping with the principles/laws of related fields such as classical mechanics, thermodynamics, and process engineering. By empirically consistent, it should be understood as the property of being consistent with the data—that is, it is confirmed by the data. Put differently, models of production should at the very least be able to be compatible with the relevant underlying laws of physics in material processes.

The inability to formally show (i.e., scientifically) how electric power–based acceleration or speed-ups increased overall productivity, thus raising the potential output of existing and new capacity, can be attributed, in large part, to the underdeveloped state of production theory both in economics and engineering. As a number of these writers pointed out, electric unit drive ushered in an age of speed, when material processes were accelerated, resulting in greater output per unit labor and capital. Process speed and acceleration, however, were absent from neoclassical production theory and process engineering.[5] Neoclassical production theory at the time focused on broadly defined capital and labor. While process engineers

[5] To be fair, process engineering was not and is not concerned with modeling wealth creation the way economics is. In fact, there are no models per se in process engineering, other than various schematics showing inputs and outputs.

were at the heart of the age of speed, their formalizations of industrial processes were, for the most part, devoid of this key element.

The Recent Literature on Productivity Growth in the 1920s and 1930s

This oversight has made for a situation in which the most recent literature (Field, 2003; Bakker et al., 2015) attributed the phenomenal growth in the 1920s and 1930s to increases in total factor productivity (TFP), which in many ways represents a setback relative to period writers who focused, for the most part, on electrification, mass production, and new power sources (see Tables 2.2 and 2.3). While the latter were unable to identify, describe, and formalize the exact transmission mechanism, they were nonetheless on the right track. The recent literature, on the other hand, contented itself with references to innovation in general (i.e., the Solow residual or TFP).

Einstein: Hopeless Confusion among Experts

Perhaps owing to his training in the natural sciences where there are few, if any, fudge factors or loose ends, Einstein felt that the debate over the causes of the Great Depression was hopelessly confused, writing, "The one thing that can encourage anyone outside the field of economics to voice an opinion on the nature of the present economic difficulties is the hopeless confusion of opinions among experts." (1932, p. 26). While he did not name names, there is every reason to believe that among the latter were a number of Europeans who had broached the topic of machinery and the business cycle, including Joseph A. Schumpeter, Nicolai

Table 2.2 Compound annual average growth rates of output per hour, private domestic and private non-farm economy, United States, 1919–1948

Period	*Private domestic economy*	*Private non-farm economy*
1919–1929	2.36	2.27
1929–1941	2.48	2.35
1941–1948	2.17	1.71

Source: Field (2003, p. 1409)

Table 2.3 TFP growth sector and industry, 1919–1929 and 1929–1941

	1919–1929		*1929–1941*	
Sector/industry	TFP	Cont.	TFP	Cont.
Private domestic economy	1.7	1.68	1.9	1.87
Manufacturing	4.5	1.18	2.3	0.61
Nonmanufacturing	0.6		1.8	1.26
One big wave sectors	2.6	0.60	3.1	0.74
Chemicals	7.6	0.21	0.70	0.02
Chemicals	7.1	0.08	2.1	0.03
Petroleum, coal products	8.2	0.10	−1.1	−0.01
Rubber products	7.3	0.03	1.5	0.01
Electricity	2.6	0.07	4.9	0.15
Electric machinery	3.1	0.03	4.6	0.05
Electric utilities	2.3	0.04	0.51	0.10
Internal combustion engine	1.9	0.30	3.30	0.54
Transport equipment	7.9	0.14	3.5	0.07
Local transit	3.6	0.04	0.4	0.00
Distribution	0.9	0.12	3.4	0.46
Communications	2.0	0.02	2.5	0.04
Telephone	1.1	0.01	1.4	0.01
Spectator equipment	3.2	0.02	4.4	0.02

Source: Bakker et al. (2015), p. 23

Kondratiev, Karl Rodbertus, and Emil Lederer, to name a few.[6] All were invariably focused on the effects of machinery. For example, nineteenth-century political economist Karl Rodbertus argued that while machinery increases productivity and output, wages are driven by the "iron law" of subsistence, leading to underconsumption.[7]

Much like contemporary growth theory where technology is essentially a nondescript variable, formalized (fittingly) and estimated as a residual, they, like Einstein, failed to go beyond the generic "technological progress" or "innovation." The next chapter fills in this void by explicitly incorporating the role of machine speed and acceleration in a model of wealth-generating material processes. Drawing from the laws of kinetics, it

[6] Beaudreau (2001) argued that the origins of Joseph Schumpeter's notion of creative destruction lay in the development of electric-magnetic power (i.e., creation) in the late nineteenth century which rendered the traditional belting, gearing, and shafting redundant (i.e., destruction).

[7] See Schumpeter (1928), Kondratieff (1926), Rodbertus (1850), and Lederer (1925).

shows how and why output and productivity are increasing in machine speed, itself the result of greater kinetic energy.

If nothing else, Einstein's remarks are indicative of a keen interest on his part in the economic matters of the day. It bears noting that the 1920s in Germany were years of economic tumult owing in large measure to the aftermath of World War I, specifically the consequences of the punitive Treaty of Versailles, which imposed heavy reparations on Germany. Subsequent restrictive tariff measures adopted by the USA (Forney-McCumber Tariff Act of 1922, Smoot-Hawley Tariff Act of 1930) and other countries, however, hampered Germany's ability to earn foreign currencies with which to meet their obligations under the treaty. Add to this the fact that it was in the process of rebuilding its war-torn economy with the latest, high-throughput, mass production techniques.[8]

Historical Antecedents

As it turns out, the debate over machinery, specifically the introduction of new machinery, and the business cycle is as old as political economy itself. It goes back to the early nineteenth century and pitted the likes of French economist Jean-Baptiste Say and David Ricardo against Jean-Charles-Léonard Simonde de Sismondi, Thomas Malthus, and British industrialist Robert Owen.[9] Like Einstein's contemporaries, they all referred to "machinery," which should be understood as a reference to the Watt-Boulton steam engine. As most were trained in moral philosophy, they were unable to provide a natural philosophy-based (read: science-based) account of the change—something we do in this book.[10]

Summary and Conclusions

This chapter presented the period and contemporary literature on productivity growth in the 1920s and 1930s. Also included was a sample of newspaper articles on electric unit drive and its effects on operating speeds and productivity. What stands out is the extent to which the two literatures are

[8] The Dawes Plan of 1924 and the Young Plan of 1929 injected much needed capital in the manufacturing sector, leading to its revival.

[9] For more on the role of energy and physics in early nineteenth-century economic thought, see Beaudreau (1998, 2025).

[10] Among the early descriptors provided were concepts such as "fire power" or "scientific power."

synoptic in their views of the paradigm of technological change that defined the 1920s and 1930s. Taken as a whole, they corroborate the first of Einstein's basic premises, namely, the presence of significant "technical progress." We now turn to the second, which consists of showing how and why this ultimately led to the downturn. This will involve presenting a model of material processes that incorporates acceleration and machine speed, the predictions of which will then be integrated into a simple macroeconomic model.

References

Bakker, G., Crafts, N., & Woltjer, P. (2015). *A vision of the growth process in a technologically progressive economy: The United States, 1929–1941* (p. 10995). CEPR.

Beaudreau, B. C. (1996). *Mass production, the stock market crash, and the great depression: The macroeconomics of electrification*. Greenwood Press.

Beaudreau, B. C. (1998). *Energy and organization: Growth and distribution Reexamined*. Greenwood Press.

Beaudreau, B. C. (2001). The origins of creative destruction. In V. Orati & S. B. Dahiya (Eds.), *Economic theory in the light of Schumpeter's scientific heritage*. Spellbound Publications.

Beaudreau, B. C. (2025). *Economics as science, a critical history of economic thought*. Taylor and Francis Routledge.

Bohn, F., & Ely, R. T. (1935). *The great change: Work and wealth in the new age*. T. Nelson and Sons.

Brookings, R. E. (1932). *The way forward*. The MacMillan Co.

Chandler, A. D. (1977). *The visible hand: The managerial revolution in American business*. Harvard University Press.

Chase, S. (1934). *The economy of abundance*. The John Day Company.

Cohen, A. (1984). Technical change as historical process: The case of the U.S. pulp and paper industry, 1915–1940. *Journal of Economic History, 44*(3), 775–799.

Devine, W. D., Jr. (1983). From shafts to wires: Historical perspective on electrification. *The Journal of Economic History, 43*, 347–372.

Devine, W. D., Jr. (1990). Electrified mechanical drive: The historical power distribution revolution. In S. H. Schurr, C. C. Burwell, W. D. Devine Jr., & S. Sonenblum (Eds.), *Electricity in the American Economy: Agent of technological Progress*. Greenwood Press.

Einstein, A. (1932). The way to a new prosperity! *Nash's Pall Mall, 52-53*, 114–115.

Field, A. J. (2003). The most technologically progressive decade of the century. *American Economic Review, 93*(4), 1399–1413.

Filene, E. A. (1923). The minimum wage and efficiency. *American Economic Review, 13*, 411–415.

Fisher, I. (1930). *The stock market crash– and after*. The Macmillan Company.

Ford, H. (1926a). *Today and tomorrow*. Doubleday.

Ford, H. (1926b). Mass production. *Encyclopaedia Britannica, 13*, 821–823.

Foster, W. T., & Catchings, W. (1927). *Business without a buyer*. Houghton Mifflin.

Giedion, S. (1948). *Mechanization takes command*. Oxford University Press.

Kondratieff, N. A. (1926). *The long waves in economic life*. The Institute for Business Cycle Research.

Laing, G. (1933). *Towards technocracy*. Angelus Press.

Lederer, E. (1925). Konjunktur und Krisen (Business Cycles and Crises). In *Grundriss der Sozialökonomik*. J.C.B. Mohr.

Lorant, J. H. (1967). Technological change in American manufacturing during the 1920s. *The Journal of Economic History, 27*(2), 243–246.

Oshima, H. T. (1984). The growth of U.S. factor productivity: The significance of new technologies in the early decades of the twentieth century. *Journal of Economic History, 44*(1), 161–170.

Polakov, W. N. (1933). *The power age, its quest and challenge*. Covici, Friede Publishers.

Rodbertus, J. K. (1850). *Sociale Briefe an von Kirchmann*. (Social Letters to von Kirchmann). Gerhard.

Schumpeter, J. A. (1928). The instability of capitalism. *The Economic Journal, 38*(151), 361–386.

Scott, H., et al. (1933). *Introduction to technocracy*. The John Day Company.

Sonenblum, S. (1990). Electrification and productivity growth in manufacturing. In S. H. Schurr, C. C. Burwell, W. D. Devine Jr., & S. Sonenblum (Eds.), *Electricity in the American Economy: Agent of technological Progress*. Greenwood Press.

Soule, G. (1947). *Prosperity decade: From war to depression 1917–1929*. Rinehart and Company.

Thomas, W. (1928). The economic significance of the increased efficiency of American industry. *American Economic Review, 18*(1), 122–138.

Tryon, F. G. (1927). An index of consumption of fuels and water power. *Journal of the American Statistical Association, 22*(2), 271–282.

Tugwell, R. G. (1927). *Industry's coming of age*. Columbia University Press.

Wright, G. (1990). The origins of American industrial success, 1879–1940. *American Economic Review, American Economic Association, 80*(4), 651–668.

CHAPTER 3

A Kinetics-Based Approach to Modeling Production

Abstract This chapter presents the kinetics-based approach to modeling production developed in Beaudreau (2020), which focuses on the role of machine speed as a key factor in productivity and growth. Drawing from the law of kinetics, it shows that output at the plant level increases at the square root of power use, providing a framework to understand the massive increase in power use in the United States in the 1910s and 1920s.

Keywords Law of kinetics • Machine speed • Acceleration • Productivity

The Speed Which Power Has Added to Production.

Characteristic also has been the rise in the use of power – three and three-quarters times faster than the growth of population – and the extent to which power has been made readily available not alone for driving tools of increasing size and capacity, but for a convenient diversity of purposes in the smallest business enterprise and on the farm and in the home. Factories no longer need to cluster about the source of power. Widespread interconnection between power plants, arising out of an increasing appreciation of the value of flexibility in power, and made possible by technical advances during recent years, has created huge reservoirs of power so that abnormal conditions in one locality need not stop the wheels of industry.

B. C. Beaudreau, *Energy, Einstein, and the Great Depression*,
https://doi.org/10.1007/978-3-032-26664-4_3

Report of President Herbert Hoover's Committee on Recent Economic Changes 1929

Introduction

As mentioned in the Introduction, the irony of Albert Einstein's foray into the debate over the causes of the Great Depression was his failure (or inability) to apply—as in, to invoke—the principles of basic mechanics to the question at hand, namely, understanding the massive increase in conventionally defined productivity in the US economy in the 1920s (i.e., in terms of labor and/or capital). As is the case with all material processes, an increase in work invariably requires an increase in energy. That is, an increase in output requires an increase in the only physically productive input, energy.

When he pointed out that "the greatest practical benefit which all these inventions confer on man is the fact that they liberate him from the excessive muscular drudgery that was once indispensable for the preservation of bare existence (Einstein 1950, p. 135)," he was abstracting from the most elementary of the laws of physics. If human beings were no longer providing muscular drudgery (force), then who or what was? Wealth being a material process, something, some force had to be doing the work.[1]

In Beaudreau (2020, 2023), it was shown that the key technological innovation/development in the 1920s was the widespread adoption of electric unit drive which allowed companies to accelerate their operating speeds, thus resulting in the spectacular growth in productivity and potential output in the 1920s. Hence, it was not the fact that muscular energy/drudgery was being replaced by electric power, but that electric unit drive, by increasing operating speeds, increased output per unit of capital/labor and reduced the demand for what Alfred Marshall referred to as "machine operatives." Put differently, acceleration and speed, two concepts at the core of Einstein's theory of relativity, were driving productivity and hence

[1] One could go as far as to argue that by the 1910s, workers had been relieved of the "drudgery" Einstein referred to. At the time, most material processes were powered by steam power delivered via belting, gearing, and shafting. The technical progress that characterized, to the point of defining, the 1920s was the conversion to electric unit drive that increased the operating speed of tools and equipment. Labor's role was largely unaffected other than being called upon to oversee or operate faster machines.Judging from his writings, his understanding of "technical progress" was mid-nineteenth century.

the rated production capacity in the US economy—that is, output when all material processes are operating at their maximum speed.

To see just how this played out, this chapter presents a physics-based model of wealth creation, which in the next chapter is integrated into a simple macroeconomic model.[2] The latter will then be used to shed light on Einstein's diagnosis as well as his prognosis. We begin with a description of the role of kinetics in material processes.

Understanding Acceleration

In physics, acceleration and speed are understood in terms of the laws of kinetics: Speed is an increasing function of kinetic energy or energy/power. In other words, acceleration is the result of greater kinetic energy. Hence, it stands to reason that an understanding of the role of acceleration in wealth creation would require, first and foremost, a model of production that incorporates speed and thus energy.

Following Beaudreau (1998), who classified factor inputs in terms of two main categories, namely, broadly defined energy and broadly defined organization, a two-tiered approach to understanding production is presented. The first tier is purely physical and is governed by the laws of physics, specifically, the laws of machine and chemical kinetics. Neither tools and/or equipment nor conventionally defined labor (supervisors) are physically productive and hence are parametric to this tier. Tier I is universal in its application and breadth, accessible to industrial engineers, to physicists, and to economists and production specialists, thus ensuring both internal and external validity. The second tier is the organization tier, which focuses on the creation and supervision of first tier material processes. It focuses on the creation and the overseeing—in short, the organization—of machines. Alfred Marshall referred to the latter in 1890 as "machine operatives." It is important to point out that such operatives are not a source of power/energy and are not physically productive; hence, they cannot be substituted for primary power. Traditional factor substitution is, as such, rendered unfeasible and theoretically impossible across our

[2] The model is an adaptation of the energy-organization model developed in Beaudreau (1998) where wealth is modeled as an increasing function of broadly defined energy and broadly defined organization, the latter being defined as the physical setting in which energy transforms as is defined in terms of tools, supervision (machine operatives and management), and information. Here, Tier I corresponds to the physical properties of material processes, while Tier II corresponds to their organizational properties. See also Beaudreau (2020).

Table 3.1 Manufacturing processes and corresponding kinetics

Type	*Kinetic law*	*Examples*	*Acceleration*
Mechanical-translational	Translational kinetics	Material handling	Higher speed
	KE = $1/2mv^2$	Transportation	
Mechanical-rotational	Rotational kinetics	Grinding, shaping	Higher speed
	KE = $1/2mi^2$	Assembling, reducing	
Chemical/thermal	Chemical kinetics	Refining, electrolysis	Higher temperature
	$k(t) = ae - Ea/RT$	Cracking	Higher voltage

two tiers. Machinery and equipment and machine operatives, not being sources of power, cannot be substituted for energy.[3]

Tier I: Machine and Chemical Kinetics at the Process and Plant Levels

A firm will be defined as a series of n sub-processes which can be of two types, namely, mechanical (n^m) and chemical (n^c) (Eq. 4.1). These are described in detail in Table 3.1. Mechanical sub-processes are governed by the laws of translational and rotational kinetics, while chemical sub-processes are governed by the laws of chemical kinetics. Included in the mechanical sub-process category are the material handling processes (pumps, conveyor belts, etc.) between the various sub-processes. That is, in sequential production processes, the output of one sub-process becomes the input for the next sub-process:

$$y(t) = \min\left[y_i^m(t)\forall i = 1,2,\ldots\ldots,n^m : y_i^c(t)\forall i = 1,2,\ldots\ldots,n^c\right] \quad (3.1)$$

Mechanical sub-processes are assumed to be governed by the laws of basic machine kinetics (translational and rotational), according to which output $y_i^m(t)$ is an increasing function of operating speed(s) $s_i^m(t)$ and

[3] While this result will appear counterintuitive to economists, it will come as no surprise to applied physicists, process engineers, and material scientists, highlighting the chasm between the two groups who nonetheless share the same goal, that of describing and understanding production processes.

the machines themselves, denoted by $k_i^m(t)$. The measured individual *n* machine speeds, defined as the machine rates of output per unit time, are governed by translational/rotational kinetics $e = 1/2mv^2$, where e = kinetic energy, m = mass, and v = velocity. As a result, in the absence of machine downtime, the effect of an increase in energy use on operating speed and hence on output will be determined by the law of translational/rotational kinetics:

$$y_i^m(t) = s_i^m(t)k_i^m(t) = e_i^m(t)^{0.5} k_i^m(t) \tag{3.2}$$

However, in the presence of machine downtime, the statistical or measured relationship between energy (e) and output $y_i^m(t)$ will be described by Eq. 3.2, where $\gamma_i^m(t)\forall i = 1,2,3,\ldots,n^m$, where $0 \le \gamma_i^m(t) \le 0.5$ is an adjustment factor. Translational kinetics defines operating speed (e.g., revolutions per minute, feet per minute) for a given mass (m) and kinetic energy (e).[4] Machine downtime can be the result of either (*i*) maintenance, (*ii*) idleness due to lack of coordination between sub-processes, or (*iii*) retooling for a new product. To capture these effects, statistical operating speed will be defined in terms of Eq. 3.3, where $\gamma_i^m(t) \ni \left[0 < \gamma_i^m(t) < 0.5\right]$ captures sub-process *i* downtime in period *t*.[5] The closer $\gamma_i^m(t)$ is to 0.5, the higher is the average downtime per *t*, and hence, the higher will be the resulting output elasticity.[6]

$$s_i^m(t) = e_i^m(t)^{0.5+\gamma_i^m(t)} \forall i = 1,2,3,\ldots,n^m \tag{3.3}$$

Thermal and chemical sub-processes (see Table 2.1) are governed by the laws of chemical kinetics (e.g., Arrhenius equation), according to which chemical reaction rates are an increasing function of temperature T_i^c which in turn is a function of energy consumption, where E_i^c is the activation energy and R is the activation energy constant (8.314) (Eq. 3.4):

[4] Machine speed can be defined either in time or in number of product (i.e., maximum speed is 10 seconds per product, maximum speed is six products per minute).

[5] In the case in which energy per machine remains constant, a one percent increase in downtime will increase output by one percent. Electric use will rise by one percent as a result. We capture this process via $\gamma(t)$.

[6] This owes to the fact that the increased energy use from restarting idle machines will result in more output than increasing energy use (i.e., increasing speed) of operating machines.

$$s_i^c(t)=\left[A_i^c \exp^{-E_i^c/RT\left(e_i^c(t)\right)}, \gamma_i^c(t)\right] \forall i=1,2,\ldots..,n^c \tag{3.4}$$

As in the previous case, temperature T is increasing energy use $e_i^c(t)$, which will result in a higher reaction rate, which in our analysis is akin to an increase in machine speed:

$$y_i^c(t)=k_i^c(t)\left[A_i^c \exp^{-E_i^c/RT\left(e_i^c(t)\right)}\right] \forall i=1,2,\ldots..,n^c \tag{3.5}$$

As was the case with mechanical sub-processes, the effect of increased energy use on operating speed (reaction rates) will be determined by two factors, namely, chemical kinetics (Arrhenius' law) and machine downtime $\gamma_i^c(t) \forall i=1,2,3,\ldots.,n^c$, where $0 \le \gamma_i^c(t) \le 0.5$.

The more downtime there is, the more linear the relationship will be, and vice versa. Equations 3.3 and 3.4 describe the two types of sub-process production functions, the first for rotation- and translation-based processes and the second for chemical- and thermal-based processes.

Assume that $s_i^m(t)$ and $s_i^c(t)$ are bounded from above. In other words, for each sub-process, there exists a maximum speed.[7] It can be defined as a combination of (*i*) translational/rotational chemical kinetics, (*ii*) material tolerances, and (*iii*) average downtime (owing to maintenance, retooling, etc).

Equations 3.2 and 3.3 define the sub-process/process technologies of a firm at time *t*. What is immediately obvious is that the speed of production at the plant level—and hence, the overall measured productivity—will depend on the n^c and n^m sub-process machine speeds—and in particular on the slowest of these sub-process speeds.[8] They also illustrate a key result, notably the explicit relationship between energy use and the

[7] $s_i(t)^{\max}=\overline{s}_i$ can be viewed as a combination of the asymptote of $s_i(t)=e_i(t)^{0.5+\gamma_i(t)} \forall i=1,2,3,\ldots.,n$ and the physical upper limits of machine speed/chemical reaction rates.

[8] In this case, machine speed defines total factor productivity—or capital productivity. It is important to keep in mind that in modern material processes, labor is a supervisory input. Hence, faster machines will raise output per unit labor (supervisory) input, despite what is essentially a constant effort on its part.

corresponding process speeds/reaction rates. Specifically, it increases quadratically—that is, doubling speed will quadruple energy consumption.[9]

These equations provide a formalization of the West's experience with energy-based technologies in the early twentieth century. As indicated by the quotations in Chap. 2, rising productivity was associated with greater energy use per unit of capital, with the latter operating on the former via the increased operating speeds made possible by electric unit drive. As Alfred Chandler pointed out, the productivity gains of the early twentieth century owed in large measure to increasing machine speeds (Jerome, 1934; Chandler, 1977, Devine, 1983). As early as 1901, Professor F.B. Crocker summarized the effect of electric unit drive on productivity and output as follows:

> *It is found that the output of manufacturing establishments is materially increased in most cases by the use of electric driving. It is often found that the gain actually amounts to 20-30 percent or even more, with the same floor space, machinery, and number of workmen. This is the most important advantage of all, because it secures an increase in income without an increase in investment, labor, or expense except perhaps for materials. In many cases, the output is raised and at the same time, the labor item is reduced. [Devine,* 1990, *p. 32]*

Sidney Sonenblum described the shift to electric unit drive from 1920 to 1948 as a period of "accelerating the rate of throughput."

> *During these years the focus of managerial attention shifted from enlarging the scale of operations to increasing operating efficiency by speeding up the rate of throughput in the plant. High priority was assigned to modifications of factory design and layout in order to better integrate worker and machine tasks. Advances in the electrification of machine drive were indispensable to the realization of these new objectives and may, indeed, have served to stimulate the new managerial perspectives that emerged. [Sonenblum,* 1990, *p. 291]*

[9] This is also the case for chemical and thermal processes, where increasing operating temperatures will increase the rate of output, but at a decreasing rate.

Tier II: Organization and the Demand for Supervision and Tools

While early nineteenth-century models of production (i.e., classical production theory) viewed labor as being physically productive (e.g., classical theory of value), by the end of the century, most mainstream economists, including neoclassical writers, viewed labor for what it had become, namely, what Alfred Marshall in 1890 referred to as "machine operatives." Take, for example, the following excerpt from Alfred Marshall's *Principles of Economics* where he refers to workers (conventional labor) as "managers":

> *We may now pass to the effects which machinery has in relieving that excessive muscular strain which a few generations ago was the common lot of more than half the working men even in such a country as England . . . in other trades, machinery has lightened man's labours. The house carpenters, for instance, make things of the same kind as those used by our forefathers, with much less toil for themselves . . . . Nothing could be more narrow or monotonous than the occupation of a weaver of plain stuffs in the old time. But now, one woman will manage four or more looms, each of which does many times as much work in the course of a day as the old hand loom did; and her work is much less monotonous and calls for much more judgment than his did. (Marshall,* 1890, *p. 218)*

This change was echoed in official statistics. For example, the UK Board of Trade, in its *Censuses of Production*, no longer referred to workers or production workers, but rather to operatives. The concept of labor productivity, it therefore follows, took on a new meaning, specifically as a measure of output per machine manager or operative. Theoretically, labor was no longer physically responsible for/involved in generating wealth, but rather was assigned the task of overseeing/managing the corresponding machines. To formalize this, the demand for supervision/machine operatives is modeled as a function of output, specifically desired output. The greater the desired or targeted level of output on the part of firms, the greater the demand for supervision and supervisors.

As machine operatives are involved in all n-sub-processes defined by Eq. 3.1, it stands to reason that the demand for supervision will depend on a number of considerations, from the individual sub-process supervision technology, to average overall machine speed, to the overall scale of operation. For example, if a company automates a given sub-process, then it would stand to reason that the demand for supervision per unit of output would fall as a result. The same would hold for an increase in machine speed, in which case machine operatives would be overseeing what a faster machine is. Only with an increase in the overall scale of operations (i.e., all sub-processes are increased by the same factor) will the demand for supervision per unit of output stay the same:

$$n(t) = \alpha\left[s(t), i(t)\right]y(t) \tag{3.6}$$

The firm-level demand for supervision can be formalized as Eq. 3.6, where n_t refers to the number of machine operatives or supervisors and α refers to the demand for supervision per unit y_t, which is a function of $s(t)$, average machine speed at time t, and $i(t)$, the level of automation at time t.[10] As such, an increase in s_t, machine speed, will result in an increase in y_t per unit n_t. However, it bears reminding that such an increase owes in no measure to labor's intrinsic properties or productivity, but rather to greater machine speed and more output per unit capital (i.e., machinery) and supervision.[11]

Similarly, information and communication technology–based technological change will affect labor demand. Specifically, innovations in machine control technology will, in general, reduce α, thus reducing the demand for supervision per unit output—in some cases, reducing it to zero (i.e., the case of total factory automation). Measured output per machine operative will, consequently, rise, again in no part due to the intrinsic contribution of conventionally defined labor:

$$k(t) = \beta\left[s(t), \eta(t)\right]y(t) \tag{3.7}$$

Like the supervisory input, tools (capital) are considered to be an organizational input, one that defines a given material process, but not one that is physically productive. According to classical mechanics, tools provide mechanical advantage, which is defined as the advantage gained by the use of a mechanism in transmitting force—specifically, the ratio of the force that performs the useful work of a machine to the force that is applied

[10] In this section, we chose to examine the demand for supervision at the more aggregate level—that is, not at the individual sub-process level.

[11] As such, it is by no means clear that labor's remuneration should rise as a result. If anything, there is reason to believe that it would decrease globally as less supervision is required for a given level of output.

to the machine. The demand for tools can, as such, be modeled analogously to that of supervision—that is, as a function of projected output, $y(t)$. According to Eq. 3.7, the demand for tools is an increasing function of the latter variable, with $\beta[s(t),\eta(t)]$ being the corresponding scaler. As can be seen, the per unit output demand for tools (capital) is a decreasing function of machine speed and, of $\eta(t)$, the level of second-law efficiency (in short, the productivity of energy). The more efficient the energy input, the less capital is required per unit output.

The Only Scientifically Possible Non-Speed-Related Process Innovation

This framework does more than just further our understanding of speed- and acceleration-based process innovations. In fact, it provides a guide of sorts to the set of theoretically feasible process innovations. Specifically, the only possible non-speed- and non-acceleration-based process innovation in an industrial setting is an increase in second-law efficiency. That is, the efficiency with which energy does work. According to our framework, this can result from either a capital-based innovation or a supervisory-based innovation. A good example of the former is James Watt's external condenser, which tripled the efficiency of the Newcomen atmospheric steam engine. An example of a supervisory-based innovation would be an improved information feedback technology that minimizes machine downtime.

Summary and Conclusions

This chapter, one could argue, has Einsteinized production theory by explicitly modeling the role of speed and acceleration in wealth-creating material processes and sub-processes. In essence, productivity as measured by output divided by either labor or capital is increasing in the operating speeds of the underlying sub-processes and processes. In the next chapter, an aggregate measure of the economy-wide level of operating speeds is incorporated into a macroeconomic model of the US economy in the 1920s.

Appendix 1: Einstein on Wealth-Creating Material Processes

One of the vexing things about the current literature on technological change—or technical progress—and its role in the Great Depression is its vagueness, its nondescript nature, and its glaring lack of precision. Just what were the innovations, the main technological advances that increased productivity manifold, leading to the worst downturn in all of history?

This is all the more damning given that material process technology is not beyond today's scientific reach—say, unlike subatomic particle physics. It's something out in the open, used on a daily basis, described in the trade and engineering journals. Yet the best period writers could do was to refer to "technical progress" or "technological change."

Table 3.2 presents a non-exhaustive listing of Einstein's descriptions of either technical progress or its effects, the latter providing some evidence as to the former.

What stands out in his writings is the recurrent reference to the notion of "technical progress removing the drudgery of human labor." From this, it can be deduced/inferred that the technical progress in question had to do with physical labor and ultimately muscular energy—less of it. It follows from classical mechanics and thermodynamics that the progress he was describing would have invariably involved an alternative energy source, one many times greater. In short, basic physics—less human force, more inanimate force. Yet, unlike Irving Fisher who focused on purchased power, Einstein makes no mention of force, let alone electric unit drive.

If anything, his account of technical progress and its effects can best be described as having a distinct Marxian undertone, specifically its similarity

Table 3.2 Einstein's description of technical progress

Definition	*Source*
Rapid progress of production methods	Way to new prosperity, *pall mall magazine*
Technical progress	Ibid
The improvement in the apparatus of production through technical invention and organization	World ills laid to machines By einstein in Berlin speech
Industrial technique	Ibid
Improvement of the mechanical apparatus and the organization	Letter to Irving fisher

to the labor theory of value. Put differently, it has a mid-nineteenth-century flavor, a time when the Watts-Boulton steam engine was replacing workers—inanimate energy sources were replacing muscular ones.

The problem is that by the 1920s, the conversion to inanimate power sources, notably the steam engine, to drive material processes had been more-or-less completed.[12] Nineteenth-century political economist Alfred Marshall went so far as to redefine workers as machine operatives.

It therefore follows that, theoretically speaking, the only possible source of higher "machine operative" productivity would be increased operating speeds—in short, acceleration. In other words, it was not the introduction of an inanimate energy source, but an increase in energy use via greater operating speeds. That Einstein was unable to come to what is an elementary result is somewhat puzzling.

Confusion over Material Processes: The Debate Degenerates

As pointed out, technology in early twentieth-century political economy was a black box of sorts, nondescript, open-ended, and all-encompassing. As it turned out, that this was the case in the 1930s would add to the confusion—among physicists. As Arthmar and Boianovsky (2024) pointed out, Einstein's lecture at Caltech in 1933 on the economic crisis (which was at its zenith by then) prompted rebuttals from a number of scholars, including his host physicist and Nobel Prize laureate Robert Millikan who argued that "technological unemployment is a myth" and that "science makes jobs and does not end them" (Arthmar & Boianovsky, 2024, p. 26).

Absent from this exchange was the basic distinction between process and product innovation. Clearly, new products can be "job-making," but new processes can be "job-ending." The point here is that the debate, even among Nobel Prize laureates, was muddled and confusing, lacking in rigor, not unlike the current debate in growth theory over the equally nondescript Solow residual.[13]

[12] The technical progress described here is acceleration-based, namely, a conversion from belting-, gearing-, and shafting-based power transmission to electro-magnetic-based transmission which allowed for greater and greater process speeds. Ultimately, the prime mover remained the same, namely, fossil fuels (other than hydro power). Thermal power plants generated kWhs that were then distributed via public utilities to both producers and consumers.

[13] In mainstream growth theory, few writers make a distinction between product and process innovation, lumping the two together in a catch-all variable, namely, research and development.

Appendix 2: Why Acceleration Is the Only Possible Long-Term Productivity-Increasing Process Innovation

The upshot of this chapter extends beyond the technological innovation in the 1920s and 1930s and beyond Einstein's writings on the causes of the Great Depression. In fact, it generalizes to all of technological innovation in the Industrial Age—an age best described as the age of speed. It explains the First Industrial Revolution as well as the Second. The Watt-Boulton dual-acting reciprocating engine increased conventionally defined productivity by accelerating the various machines and processes of the day. In short, virtually all of the artisanal (i.e., muscle powered) were speeded and could be operated continually (24/7). Innovations in steam-generating technology (e.g., high-pressure steam, steam turbines) allowed for greater and greater operating speeds.

According to basic physics, energy and energy alone is physically productive. Machinery and equipment, as well as the operator (i.e., of the machinery and equipment), are organizational inputs, defining the framework or context in which power performs work—in this case, creates wealth. Theoretically speaking, the latter affect productivity via their effect on second-law efficiency. A good example is James Watt's original external condenser, which raised the efficiency of the Newcomen steam engine by a factor of three—by reducing heat loss. Given that second-law efficiency is bounded from above, it stands to reason that, theoretically speaking, such gains are limited. In short, it is highly stable across material processes.

This leaves acceleration, powered by greater and greater amounts of energy, as the only theoretically possible long-term productivity-increasing process innovation. While to many, this will appear to be overly restrictive, the historical record speaks for itself. All of the major gains in wealth creation in the modern era have resulted from our ability to accelerate known material processes.

References

Arthmar, R., & Boianovsky, M. (2024). Einstein, Fisher, science and the great depression. *The European Journal of the History of Economic Thought, 31*(6), 948–975.

Beaudreau, B. C. (1998). *Energy and organization: Growth and distribution Reexamined*. Greenwood Press.

Beaudreau, B. C. (2020). *The economics of speed: Machine speed as the key factor in productivity*. Springer.

Beaudreau, B. C. (2023). *The great depression, its origins in acceleration and electric unit drive*. World Scientific.

Chandler, A. D. (1977). *The visible hand: The managerial revolution in American business*. Harvard University Press.

Devine, W. D., Jr. (1983). From shafts to wires: Historical perspective on electrification. *The Journal of Economic History, 43*, 347–372.

Devine, W. D., Jr. (1990). Electrified mechanical drive: The historical power distribution revolution. In S. H. Schurr, C. C. Burwell, W. D. Devine Jr., & S. Sonenblum (Eds.), *Electricity in the American Economy: Agent of technological Progress*. Greenwood Press.

Einstein, A. (1950). *Out of my later years*. Philosophical Library.

Jerome, H. (1934). *Mechanization in industry*. National Bureau of Economic Research.

Marshall, A. (1890). *Principles of economics*. Macmillan.

Sonenblum, S. (1990). Electrification and productivity growth in manufacturing. In S. H. Schurr, C. C. Burwell, W. D. Devine Jr., & S. Sonenblum (Eds.), *Electricity in the American Economy: Agent of technological Progress*. Greenwood Press.

CHAPTER 4

A Macroeconomic Model of the US Economy with Acceleration

Abstract This chapter integrates the kinetics approach to modeling material processes into a simple macroeconomic model of the economy and examines the impacts of acceleration on productivity, output, and employment. This provides a theoretical framework in which to examine Einstein's many predictions of the effects of technical progress on the economy. It also examines the validity of many of his policy recommendations.

Keywords Macroeconomic model • Acceleration • Employment • Policy options

Introduction

One of the key elements in Einstein's writings was the need for balance—that is, balance between production and consumption. In his words, "In this way, it would probably be possible to establish an equilibrium between production and consumption without too great a restriction of free initiative and at the same time eliminate the disproportionate superiority of the owners of the means of production machinery over wage earners (in the widest sense)" (Einstein 1932, p. 2).

B. C. Beaudreau, *Energy, Einstein, and the Great Depression*,
https://doi.org/10.1007/978-3-032-26664-4_4

Interestingly but not surprisingly, this was also one of the key findings of President Hoover's *Report on Recent Economic Changes* published in 1929, which was prepared by engineers, civil servants, and economists. That the engineers opted to use the term "balance" as opposed to "equilibrium" can be attributed to their lack of formal training in economics. However, one could argue that balance connotes more than equilibrium—that is, in a dynamic setting.

In this chapter, a macroeconomic model which incorporates acceleration-based increases in the rated capacity of existing plant and equipment is presented and used to examine the macroeconomics of speed-increasing electric unit drive. The resulting predictions will be used to illustrate a number of Einstein's observations, notably that technological progress—in this case, the conversion to electric unit drive—led to a decrease in the level of employment and output instead of the anticipated increase in actual—not only potential—output. They will also be used to formalize and evaluate Einstein's policy recommendations.

The Breadth of EUD-Based Acceleration

The various references to electric unit drive and acceleration provided above appear to focus exclusively on the manufacturing sector. However, as the General Electric Company, in its 1937 promotional video, pointed out, the "magic of speed" was universal in its breadth, touching virtually all sectors and all types of economic activity, from manufacturing to mining, to transportation, to agriculture, to services. In short, given that virtually all forms of wealth creation are based on energy, electric unit drive, by increasing the amount of kinetic energy via acceleration and greater machine speeds, increased productivity—of existing as well as new machinery and equipment, broadly defined.

It is important to point out that not all industries and sectors were affected equally and that not all firms within the affected industries and sectors had converted to electric unit drive, giving rise to a considerable amount of heterogeneity in the economy. That being said, in this chapter, it will be assumed that machinery and equipment speed can be aggregated into a single, economy-wide measure—variable, $s(t)$.

It could be argued that most, if not all, process and product innovations in the 1920s were energy-related. Electric unit drive with its versatility (size- and HP-wise) ushered in a whole new line of products (i.e., household appliances) and processes, the latter being largely speed-based.

Table 4.1 Product innovations in the 1920s

Radio	*Traffic light*	*Penicillin*
Refrigerator	Television	Bandaid
Bulldozer	Model T automobile	Vacuum cleaner
Washing machine	Automobiles	Aviation
Electric blender	Electric razors	Insulin
Telephone	Polygraph	Water skiing
Frozen foods		

Source: https://www.google.com/search?q=product+innovations+in+the+1920s&oq=product+innovations+in+the+1920s&gs_lcrp=EgZjaHJvbWUyBggAEEUYOTIHCAEQIRigATIHCAIQIRigATIHCAMQIRigATIHCAQQIRigATIHCAUQIRifBTIHCAYQIRifBdIBCDY3NzdqMGo0qAIAsAIB&sourceid=chrome&ie=UTF-8

Table 4.1 lists product innovations in the 1920s generated randomly by Google. As can be seen, most are electricity- and/or speed-related.[1]

Model

To capture the notion of machine/process speed–related increases in aggregate potential output (Polakov, 1933; Jerome, 1934; Chandler, 1977), the left-hand side of the standard national income accounting equation was modified as shown in Eq. 4.1, where the value of aggregate output (GDP) is defined as the product of $p(t)$, the price level; $s(t)$, average economy-wide machine speed per hour (units per hour); $k(t)$, aggregate capital (plant and equipment); and $h(t)$, the average number of hours the machine/unit aggregate capital operates.[2] Average machine speed is, by definition, an aggregate of economy-wide individual machine speeds. Machines in this case include all material processes, from manufacturing to transportation, to the service sector. As labor and capital are not physically productive inputs (Beaudreau, 1998), but rather are organizational in nature, it will be assumed that regardless of $s(t)$, each unit of capital $k(t)$ requires one unit of labor $n(t)$. In other words, each unit of capital requires a single supervisor.[3]

[1] In fact, many are electric motor (electric unit drive) based. Refrigerators, washers, dryers, dishwashers, vacuum cleaners, and power tools are examples.

[2] Polakov (1933) outlined a similar model, as follows: Output=TxExR, where T=time, E=employees, and R=rate of production or machine speed.

[3] Accordingly, $k(t)h(t)$ defines the aggregate number of hours worked per day. Equivalent monthly and yearly levels can be obtained by simply scaling $k(t)h(t)$ up by the number of days (30 and 365, respectively).

$h(t)$, the average number of hours worked, is as such a measure of capacity utilization, with 24 being the maximum ($\bar{h}$) it can take on.

The right-hand side of the equation defines aggregate expenditure.[4] To simplify the analysis, it is assumed that all of the wage income is consumed and all of the profit income is invested. Purchasing power, and hence consumption expenditure, is defined as the product of $w(t)$, the average wage, and $h(t)$ and $k(t)$. If capital is fully employed, $h(t)$ would be 24, which is the equivalent of three eight-hour shifts. Overall profits $\pi^i(t)$ are defined as the sum of $\pi^v(t)$, profits that are used to finance planned investment expenditure, and $\pi^s(t)$, excess profits that are saved.[5] Put differently, investment expenditure is assumed to be exogenous, being determined at the beginning of time t ($\pi^v(t)$). Another way of seeing this is that any additional profit income (unanticipated) is not automatically invested in new capacity. Last, a discretionary expenditure variable φ is included for analytical purposes—that is, to allow for the analysis of discretionary policy measures such as tariff policy or expenditure policy[6]:

$$p(t)s(t)k(t)h(t) = w(t)k(t)h(t) + \pi^v(t) + \varphi \qquad (4.1)$$

$$h(t) = \frac{1}{\left[p(t)s(t) - w(t)k(t)\right]}\left[\pi^v(t) + \varphi\right] \qquad (4.2)$$

Solving Eq. 4.1 for $h(t)$ yields Eq. 4.2, where the equilibrium number of hours (out of a possible 24) per machine (i.e., unit of $k(t)$) is decreasing in $p(t)$ and $s(t)$, but increasing in $w(t)$. An increase in $s(t)$, the average economy-wide machine speed, will ceteris paribus decrease $h(t)$, the

[4] Implicitly, we assume a variant of Say's law, namely, that money income equals money expenditure. However, income is not always equal to potential output as defined by the left-hand side of Eq 4.1.

[5] Given that our model is based on the presence of excess rated capacity (i.e., $h(t)$ less than 24), profit income while a function of $h(t)$ will be considered a scaler in so far as its effect on expenditure is concerned. This makes for the possibility of what could be referred to as excess investment funds (i.e., $\pi^x(t) > 0$).

[6] The interest rate as a determinant of aggregate expenditure was not included, essentially for two reasons, namely, that consumer credit was not well established in the period under study and, second, the presence of significant excess capacity in the 1920s and 1930s and the corresponding low (perhaps zero) interest-rate elasticity of investment expenditure (Steindl, 2004).

average number of hours worked (Eq. 4.2).[7] This follows from the fact that increased productivity in the face of constant expenditure ($w(t)$ is fixed) will force firms to reduce the number of operating hours, thus reducing the demand for labor.[8] Einstein referred to this as "technological unemployment." However, as indicated by Eq. 4.2, if the same increase in $s(t)$ is accompanied by a commensurate increase in $w(t)$, then $h(t)$ would not be affected. As a result, overall wage income will increase, as will overall profit income. If investors use the latter to increase planned investment, then overall expenditure will increase in proportion to the increase in productive capacity—in short, the key to a successful transition.

As in the standard macroeconomic model, a decrease in planned expenditure (i.e., $[\pi^x(t) + \varphi]$) will decrease $h(t)$ via the acceleration-adjusted multiplier (i.e., $\frac{1}{\left[p(t)s(t)-w(t)k(t)\right]}$). According to the latter, an increase in $s(t)$ will diminish the efficacy of fiscal policy as every additional dollar spent will require fewer hours given the greater machine speed. Also, the acceleration-adjusted multiplier is decreasing in $w(t)$. Thus, lowering wages/falling wages in a downturn will hamper expenditure-based efforts to increase employment, which may explain why Presidents Herbert Hoover and Franklin Roosevelt were opposed to a decrease in wages to restore employment in the early years of the downturn. It also rationalizes their high-wage doctrine as higher wages increase the acceleration-adjusted multiplier.[9]

Acceleration, Disequilibrium, and Policy

In Einstein's view, the introduction of new, more efficient machines had the effect of reducing labor demand—what he referred to as "working power."[10] In his words

[7] This version of the multiplier is akin to Richard F. Kahn's, 1931 original employment multiplier. See Kahn (1931).

[8] By definition, the aggregate level of hours is simply the product of $h(t)$ and $k(t)$.

[9] This we maintain captures Keynes' argument that a decrease in wages could potentially decrease output.

[10] That he referred to labor as working power is problematic for a number of reasons. First, by 1930, most workers were, as Alfred Marshall pointed out in 1890, machine operatives. Hence, to refer to them as "power" is surprising (his only reference to energy in describing the wealth creation process). Second, the use of the word power is evidence of a quasi-rap-

> *This conviction of mine is that our present crisis does not have the character of former crises inasmuch as it is founded upon an entirely new condition, one resulting from the rapid progress of production-methods—only a fraction of the human working-power at our disposal is now necessary to produce the world's total demand for the necessities of life. The inevitable result of this is that only part of our human working-power can find utilization, in view of to-day's state of working methods. While one portion of our working-power is being unreasonably claimed—perhaps overworked—the remainder is automatically cast entirely out of the production process—left idle.*

Just how the rapid progress (i.e., acceleration) of production methods (i.e., an increase in $s(t)$) affects output and employment will depend on a number of factors, the most important of which is the choice on the part of firms whether to (i) produce at the new, higher accelerated level of output or (ii) operate plant and equipment at the new, accelerated speed but reduce the utilization rate.[11] Each is now examined.

Acceleration and Full Capacity Utilization

In this case, companies operate their plants at full capacity, which entails $h(t) = 24$ and maximum speed (i.e., $s(t)$). Hence, the left-hand side of Eq. 4.1 increases, thus creating a fundamental disequilibrium—or imbalance. Given that wages and profits have not changed, it stands to reason that product markets in general will find themselves with excess supply—that is, unsold products. It is important to remember that the investors/shareholders are not paid an ex ante salary-equivalent return on capital, but that profits (paid in the form of dividends) are paid after sales occur—as a Knightian residual. As such, the resulting imbalance or disequilibrium owes in this case not to underconsumption or underinvestment but rather to insufficient overall income and purchasing power.

prochement between economics and physics. In his view, workers were a source of the energy that powered production. However, this maintained that technical progress had increased productivity to the point that fewer workers were needed. This implies that employed workers somehow increased their worker power. Given the fact that he did not mention any other power source thus amounts to arguing that workers supplied either more of the 2000 kilocalories of their potential daily caloric energy or that the latter actually increased.

[11] A third possibility would be to maintain pre-conversion machine speeds—that is, the status quo. Technically, this is impossible with AC motors that have to be operated at their rated speeds.

Not surprisingly, this is an unlikely outcome for a number of reasons, not least the fact that firms are more likely to reduce hours before they decide to flood the market with their products. In short, it is unlikely in anything other than the context of perfectly competitive markets where the firms' demand curves are perfectly horizontal.

President Herbert Hoover's *Committee on Recent Economic Changes* was well aware of this scenario, which prompted it to focus attention on new ways in which to market goods and services. It stopped short of calling for higher wages, but did devote two chapters to the question.

Acceleration and Constrained Capacity Utilization

In this case, companies operate their plants at accelerated speeds, but reduce capacity utilization (i.e., $h(t)$). In so doing, they reduce their variable costs by roughly the same percentage as the increase in speed. For example, if speed accelerates by 20%, then the current level of output can be produced with an 80% utilization rate. In this case, $h(t)$ falls, which translates into a weakening of the level of employment and of the labor market in general. Thorstein Veblen referred to this response as a form of sabotage, as it pre-empted the full utilization of the newfound potential. Einstein referred to it as a decrease in worker power.

Unlike the previous case, here, wage income as a proportion of overall income will decrease as labor costs per unit of output decrease, resulting in a greater return to the owners of capital. However, once again, the problem lies not in the ratio of wage to profit income per se, but rather in an insufficient overall level of income.[12]

Acceleration and Underincome

Generalized, economy- and sector-wide machine speed-ups/acceleration present important challenges in so far as their income equivalents are concerned, owing in large measure to the fundamental nature of the process of income creation/generation in for-profit market economies. More specifically, as mentioned above, the resulting productivity and output gains have, according to the laws of kinetics, nothing to do with either labor or

[12] It's not clear that even if the ratio of wage to profit income was restored to the pre-technology shock era, full employment would be restored.

capital. Existing machinery and equipment is simply speeded up, and workers are called upon to oversee what are faster machines. Fundamentally, the productivity gains are the result of the increased energy consumption (i.e., according to the laws of kinetics), leading to increased process speed and increased productivity. One way of seeing this is that energy (i.e., *kWhs*) creates rents or returns which, for a successful transition, need to be (*i*) assigned/attributed and (*ii*) monetized. This could be achieved by either increasing wages and/or increasing profits.

The problem with the former lies in the fact that it cannot be justified by workers' contribution to productivity (labor being a supervisory input), making for a situation in which companies will not increase wages—or will resist increasing wages on technical grounds. Put differently, as workers' tasks will not have changed, there would be no legitimate reason to increase wages. Similarly, increasing profits is also problematic, as machinery and equipment are not the cause of the increase in output. Moreover, as profits—returns to capital—are a residual form of factor payment, paid out ex post and not ex ante, the fact that sales have not increased (and could possibly decrease) implies that profits will not increase. Theoretically, this follows from the fact that investors/shareholders are not paid a "wage" prior to the sale of the product like workers.[13]

Einstein was well aware of this conundrum. In his eyes, the problem was not one of insufficient demand per se, but of insufficient income or what he referred to as "buying power." In other words, the market fails to generate income levels commensurate with the value of GDP at current prices. In this regard, his views differ fundamentally from the traditional underconsumption literature, which focuses on expenditure, not income.[14]

> *Generally speaking, over-production signifies production of one kind of merchandise in greater quantity than can be sold under prevailing circumstances, despite the scarcity of such merchandise among consumers. I call this "apparent" over-production. In this case, it is not the demand that is lacking, but the buying power of the consumer.*

[13] As University of Chicago economics professor Frank Knight put it in 1923, shareholders are residual claimants.

[14] It bears reminding that while underincome necessarily implies underconsumption, underconsumption does not necessarily imply underincome.

Acceleration-Based Disequilibrium: A Numerical Example

Let $p(t) = 1$, $s(t) = 5$, $k(t) = 10$, $h(t) = 24$, $w(t) = 3.5$, $\pi(t) = 360$.

In this numerical example (Table 4.2), acceleration increases $s(t)$ from 5/h to 7/h, a 40% increase in period 1. Initial GDP is 1200, with a wage income of 840 and a profit income of 360. In the first iteration, output rises to 1680, which is not sustainable given income and expenditure, thus forcing firms to readjust, decreasing $h(t)$ in the second iteration to 17.14, which brings the level of output back down to 1200. However, in so doing, it reduces the wage bill to 600, thus decreasing overall expenditure to 960. In the next iteration, firms decrease $h(t)$ to 13.71 in the hope of re-equilibrating the product market. However, in so doing, wage income decreases to 480, thus forcing yet another cut in $h(t)$. This process continues until round 10, where equilibrium is reestablished as output, income, and expenditure are all equal—or in balance.

This example assumes that investment expenditure is fixed and thus not affected by the resulting downward spiral. It also highlights the fact that in the process, firms will initially earn higher profits (Column 6) as labor costs per hour (3.5) are constant despite productivity gains of 40%, but that eventually, they will return to their initial level. If this is not the case and investment decreases (the most probable scenario), then the decrease in output and employment will be greater.

Table 4.2 Acceleration-based disequilibrium: a numerical example

Period	$h(t)$	$p(t)s(t)h(t)k(t)$	$w(t)h(t)k(t)$	$\pi^{v}(t)$	$\pi^{s}(t)$
0	24	1200	840	360	0
1	24	1680	840	360	0
2	17.14	1200	600	360	240
3	13.71	960	480	360	120
4	12	840	420	360	60
5	11.14	780	390	360	30
6	10.71	750	375	360	25
7	10.50	735	367	360	8
8	10.40	728	363	360	5
9	10.33	724	361	360	3
10	10.31	722	360	360	2

Policy Options

This brings us to discuss, as did Einstein, the possible policy options. The question is the one Einstein asked himself, namely, how could the government (third party) close a technical progress—in this case, an acceleration-based output gap? In other words, what policy or policies could it pursue to restore full employment?

Consider the following non-exhaustive policy options. The first option would be to impose via legislation an increase in real wages proportional to the increase in productivity—that is, in percentage terms. For example, if acceleration increases productivity by 40%, then real wages would increase by 40%. In cases in which acceleration is not generalized, real wages would increase only in the affected firms/industries. Practically, this could be operationalized by tying real wages to increases in electric power usage per unit of capital or labor. That way, only companies and industries that are affected would see their real wage increase.[15] According to Eq. 4.2, this would increase operating rates (i.e., $h(t)$) and, ultimately, employment.

A second option would be to increase central bank-financed government expenditure in an amount of the output gap (i.e., $480). Understandably, there would be problems with this approach. First, it would serve to increase profits (residual) without increasing wages. Profits would increase as companies produce at the new, higher level of output, raising the question whether the resulting excess savings would be invested, and in so doing raise the overall level of expenditure. If not, then the initial increase in government expenditure would have to be recurrent. Year in, year out, it would need to maintain the higher level of expenditure via increased money-supply-based expenditure levels. This, in turn, would raise other issues such as the resulting increased liquidity in the banking system (owing to increased profits) and its effects on the economy.

As it turned out, Einstein struggled with this very issue, going as far as to question the ability of a market economy to maintain full employment. In his *Pall Mall* article, he suggested that the way to prevent a downturn is for the government to prevent the buying power of the masses from sinking below a certain minimum point.

[15] This was effectively the problem occasioned by President Franklin D. Roosevelt's National Industrial Recovery Act of 1933 and the President's Reemployment Act.

If in one way or another one should succeed in preventing the buying power of the masses from sinking below a certain minimum-point, measured in merchandise value, such stagnations of economic circulation as we are presently experiencing would be made impossible.

It is not clear, however, that this is the case. While doing so would prevent the downward spiral illustrated in Table 4.2, it would not restore full employment. As shown, full employment could only be achieved by increasing "the buying power of the masses" by an amount equivalent to the increase in overall productivity.

What is clear, however, is his view of the free market and its incompatibility with full employment in periods of paradigm technological change. This led him in later writings to explore alternatives, including replacing markets with government, pointing to the newly created Soviet Union and its elaborate system of economic planning. We will return to this question in Chap. 8.

Clearly, the policy options available to a government are relatively limited, other than decreeing an across-the-board increase in wages, assuming, of course, that the speed-ups are generalized across the industries and sectors of the economy. This would directly address the problem of the nonproprietary nature of the resulting energy/speed rents. Acceleration increases potential output without commensurately increasing costs and hence national income, making for a macroeconomic disequilibrium.[16] Neither labor nor capital can legitimately lay claim to these rents, yet in order to maintain a full-employment equilibrium, they must somehow be assigned/attributed/monetized. That is, the right-hand side of Eq. 4.1 must be equal to the left-hand side for a value of $h(t) = 24$.

Historical Antecedents

These allegations were not proper to twentieth-century America. In fact, identical ones had been leveled at nineteenth-century Britain with the introduction of the steam engine, which, like electric unit drive, accelerated material processes, increasing potential output 100-fold according to political economists such as David Ricardo and Thomas Malthus at the introduction of the steam engine. British industrialist turned social critic,

[16] In other words, the value of the wealth created by accelerating existing machinery and equipment exceeds by far the cost—in short, it generates energy rents.

Robert Owen, in *Report to the County of Lanark*, referred to the effect of scientific power on potential output, pointing to wage income being insufficient to take the output off the market. Similar arguments were made by Jean-Charles-Léonard Simonde de Sismondi in 1819 and Robert Thomas Malthus in 1823. Both referred to the inability of a market economy to increase wage income commensurately with productivity and potential output. Insufficient purchasing power in the face of technological change (i.e., the steam engine) was an element in Karl Marx's account of the business cycle.

Summary and Conclusions

The next chapter describes in greater detail the technical developments in the 1910s and 1920s that made the acceleration and productivity gains possible, namely, the development of electric unit drive and large-scale interconnected electrical utilities. Interestingly, both were ignored in the mainstream literature, owing no doubt to their nonmaterial nature. Power was power, whether it be generated on site and transmitted to machinery and equipment by shafts, gears, and belts or purchased from a local utility and transmitted to machinery and equipment by electric wires. Yet the difference in terms of productivity was enormous.

References

Beaudreau, B. C. (1998). *Energy and organization: Growth and distribution Reexamined*. Greenwood Press.

Chandler, A. D. (1977). *The visible hand: The managerial revolution in American business*. Harvard University Press.

Einstein, A. (1932). The way to a new prosperity! *Nash's Pall Mall, 52-53*, 114–115.

Jerome, H. (1934). *Mechanization in industry*. National Bureau of Economic Research.

Kahn, R. F. (1931). The relation of home investment to unemployment. *The Economic Journal, 41*, 173–198.

Marshall, A. (1890). *Principles of economics*. Macmillan.

Polakov, W. N. (1933). *The power age, its quest and challenge*. Covici, Friede Publishers.

Simonde de Sismondi, J. C. L. (1819). *Nouveaux Principes d'Économie Politique*. Delaunay.

Steindl, F. G. (2004). *Understanding economic recovery in the 1930s: Endogenous propagation in the great depression*. University of Michigan Press.

CHAPTER 5

Electric Unit Drive and Large-Scale Interconnected Electrical Utilities

Abstract While electric unit drive revolutionized material processes throughout the US economy, its rapid adoption owed in large measure to the development in the post-WWI period of large-scale, interconnected electrical utilities that offered virtually unlimited power at low prices, making conversion to electric unit drive all the more attractive. This chapter examines this key development in ushering in the Roaring Twenties.

Keywords Electric unit drive • Interconnection • Low-cost electric power

> *The speed with which electricity was adopted may be readily indicated. Electric motors accounted for less than 5 percent of total installed horsepower in American manufacturing in 1899. The growth in the first years of the twentieth century was such that by 1909, their share of manufacturing horsepower was 25 percent. Ten years later the share rose to 55 percent and by 1929 electric motors completely dominate the manufacturing sector by providing over 80 percent of total installed horsepower. The sharp rise in productivity in the American economy, in the years after World War I, doubtless owed a great deal, both directly and indirectly, to the electrification of manufacturing.*
>
> *Nathan Rosenberg*, 1972

B. C. Beaudreau, *Energy, Einstein, and the Great Depression*,
https://doi.org/10.1007/978-3-032-26664-4_5

Introduction

Einstein was categorical in his Nash's *Pall Mall* article:

> *In the other hand, for me it has become an established fact that the technical progress which, in itself, would be destined to relieve humanity of a large part of the burden of work necessary for its maintenance is the chief cause of our present plight. Therefore, many critics who agree with me seriously want to prohibit the introduction of more and more mechanical improvements. This is obviously nonsense. But, how can a more sensible way out of this dilemma be found?*

The introduction of large-scale, interconnected electrical utilities paved the way for what was perhaps the greatest increase in energy availability in US history, namely, the 1920s. As result of a number of legal and technical developments in the 1910s and 1920s, electric power was not only inexpensive but readily available. Companies no longer had to generate it on site but could now purchase it, making electric unit drive affordable, prompting one of the most spectacular increases in wealth in all of history, namely, the near doubling of potential output in large swathes of US industries. After all, if by converting to electric unit drive, operating speeds are doubled, potential output will also double. To set the stage, this chapter focuses on power drive technologies in general, which, by definition, consist of (*i*) the power source and (*ii*) the transmission mechanism—also known as the drive technology—and on electric unit drive in particular. The transmission mechanism is, by definition, the technology that delivers the power to the relevant tool, which, in turn, performs the work that ultimately creates wealth.[1] While electrification has a history in US manufacturing dating back to the late nineteenth century when steam engines powered shafts and belts, it was only with the introduction of unit drive that productivity soared, owing in large measure to the resulting greater machine operating speeds.

This chapter examines in greater detail the conversion to electric unit drive, focusing on the logistics, notably the power supply and conversion from the cumbersome belting, shafting, and gearing to direct drive. It also provides an estimate of the growth in power consumption and the resulting increases in productivity and output.

[1] This view is consistent with Beaudreau (1998, 2020) according to which wealth creation is an increasing function of work, which, in turn, is an increasing function of energy use.

The Role of Power Drive Technologies in Industrialization

Power drive technologies were by far the defining feature of the Industrial Revolution. James Watt and Matthew Boulton's highly successful reciprocating steam engine, patented in 1782, increased throughput rates (machine speed) multifold throughout British industry and, in so doing, led to the First Industrial Revolution.[2] Technically speaking, it increased the amount of power that could be delivered to a tool or set of tools per unit time, which, according to the laws of kinetics, resulted in greater speeds or, simply put, acceleration.[3] This was achieved by simply increasing the speed at which the shaft from the engine to the tool/machine was turning. Put differently, the First Industrial Revolution was, first and foremost, about speed—a manifold increase in the speed of the throughput and output.[4] In light of the integral role power drive technologies played and play in the creation of wealth, each element will be examined in detail.

Power Sources

By power source, it should be understood the prime movers—that is, the ultimate source of power or energy.[5] Among these are hydraulic, wind, chemical, nuclear, and solar sources. Each can be defined in terms of its ability to do or perform work. Hydraulic refers to a combination of water (H2O) and gravity. Ultimately, the force at work is gravity. Wind power refers to temperature gradients that result in pressure differences and ultimately in a source of work. Chemical energy refers to the heat energy that is released in a chemical reaction. Nuclear energy refers to the energy released in an atomic reaction, or, put simply, the ability to do work that results from such a reaction. Solar energy refers to the ability to do work from solar radiation.

Ultimately, these six power sources are tributaries of the four fundamental fields. The story of civilization, it could be argued, is the story of a

[2] In fact, one could include John Kay's Spinning Jenny in the category of power drive technologies, as a single individual could now drive multiple spindles.

[3] Tools can be simple or complex, with the latter consisting of multiple simple tools.

[4] It is important to note that the Industrial Revolution witnessed no new products per se. In other words, existing material processes (largely artisanal) were speeded up/accelerated.

[5] It is worthwhile noting that electricity is not a power source, but rather a power transmission technique.

Table 5.1 Power sources

Source	*Technology*
Hydraulic	Water wheels, water turbines
Wind	Wind mills
Chemical	Fossil fuels, wood
Nuclear/atomic	Nuclear reactors
Solar	Solar panels

species, *Homo sapiens*, and its ability to direct/use/exploit increasing quanta of the Earth's available energy. Among the key breakthroughs were the Neolithic Revolution, which witnessed the development of large-scale agriculture and the increasing use of fire to fashion tools; the Industrial Revolution, which was marked by the large-scale use of coal and coke to power material processes; and the Nuclear Age, where *Homo sapiens-sapiens* tapped into the energy stored in atoms (see Table 5.1).

Transmission Mechanisms

By definition, transmission mechanisms transmit the energy source to the tool, which ultimately performs the work. A windmill is a good example of a transmission mechanism that transmits wind energy (temperature gradient) into power that drives the grinding stones and thus mills the various grains. It consists of a series of shafts, gears, and, in some cases, pulleys. Transmission mechanisms, in general, range from shafts and belts to dynamos and electric motors. In the latter case, the source of energy is transformed into electromagnetic force, which powers AC or DC motors, which, in turn, power various tools (see Fig. 5.1 and Table 5.2).

Power Drive Technologies in the US Industry: A Timeline

Figure 5.2 presents the timeline of the drive technologies (see Table 5.2) in US manufacturing from 1869 to 1939. What stands out is the extent to which, by 1939, electric unit drive had displaced steam engines and water power as the prime mover in US manufacturing. With this shift came a decrease in capital intensity as EUD dispensed with the cumbersome—and costly—shafting and belting that had characterized mechanical drive from the get-go. More important, however, was the fact that it removed what had been, for decades, the upper limit on machine speed, thus opening the way to acceleration-based productivity and capacity increases.

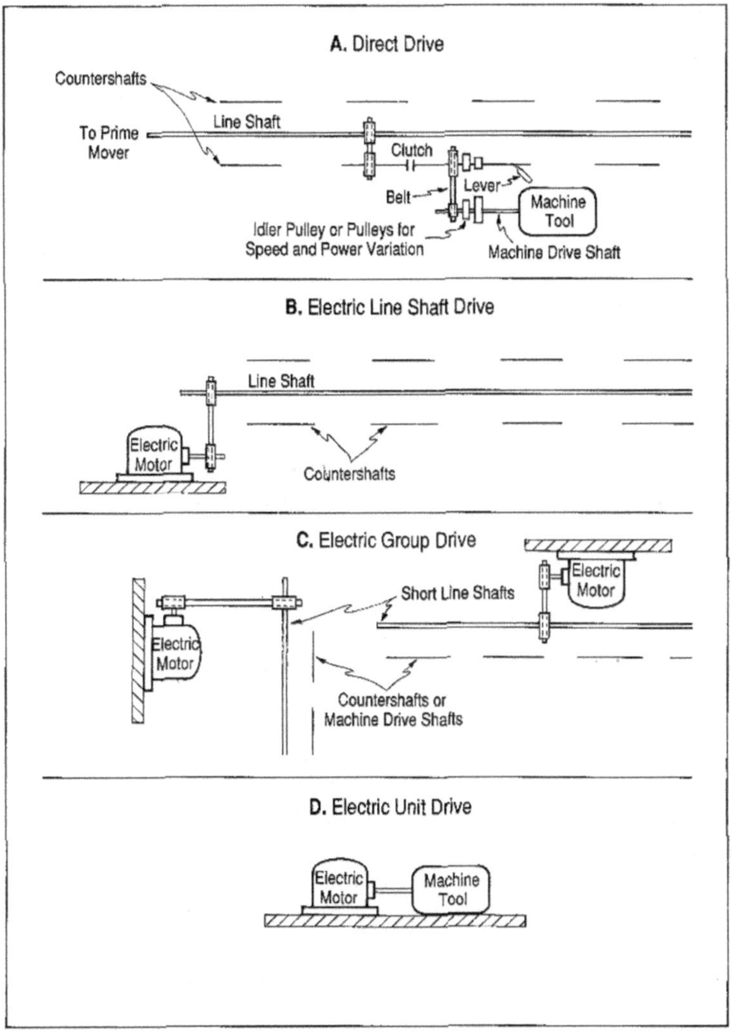

Fig. 5.1 Material process power transmission technologies

Table 5.2 Transmission mechanisms

Shafts wooden, iron, and steel
Gearing wooden, iron, and steel
Belting
Dynamos and electric motor unit versus group drive (achieved with a combination of shafts, gears, and belts)

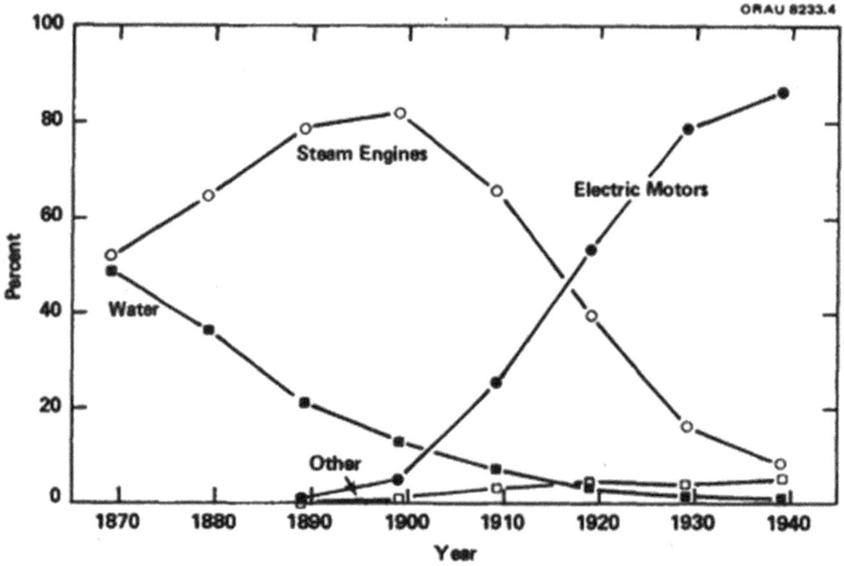

Fig. 5.2 Evolution of mechanical drive in US manufacturing

Electric Unit Drive: A Revolution in Power Drive Technology

Power drive technologies differ in the quantity of energy they can transmit to/deliver to a tool/machine per period of time. The more kinetic energy, the greater the speed of operation, and the more work that can be achieved, again per period of time. Primitive wooden gears and shafts were limited speed-wise (measured in *rpms*), largely as a result of low material tolerances. Complex belting and shafting power drive technology was also limited. As it turns out, the greatest innovation or revolution in power drive technologies occurred with the introduction of the electric unit drive.

Prior to the 1910s and 1920s, power within plants was distributed via a single shaft, which powered a series of smaller shafts, which, in turn, powered a number of belts, which ultimately powered the various tools. In addition to being cumbersome and prone to breakdown, this configuration placed an upper limit on operating speeds. In addition, a good part of the force generated by the prime mover (steam engine or electric motor) was used to drive the various gears, shafts, and belts and thus was not delivered to the tools, those being lost productivity-wise.[6] According to Warren Devine (1983)

> *It is found that the output of manufacturing establishments is materially increased in most cases by the use of electric driving. It is often found that the gain actually amounts to 20 to 30 percent or even more, with the same floor space, machinery, and number of workers. This is the most important advantage of all because it secures an increase in income without an increase in the investment, labor, or expense, except perhaps for material. In many cases, the output is raised, and at the same time, the labor item is reduced (Devine,* 1990, *p. 32)*

Sidney Sonenblum (1990) made a similar point:

> *During these years, the focus of management attention shifted from enlarging the scale of operations to increasing operating efficiency by speeding up the rate of throughput in the plant. High priority was assigned to modifications of factory design and layout in order to better integrate worker and machine tasks. Advances in the electrification of machine drive were indispensable to the realization of these new objectives and, indeed, may have served to stimulate the new managerial perspective that emerged (Sonenblum,* 1990, *p. 291)*

As it turns out, the resulting speed-based increases in wealth was nothing new, as speed had been the key element in the First Industrial Revolution as well as the subsequent increases in productivity. More specifically, the Boulton-Watt reciprocating, high-pressure steam engine, by increasing the rated capacity of existing plant and equipment, was single-handedly responsible for the manifold increase in UK wealth in the nineteenth century. Material processes that had been powered by human and animal muscles were sped up and operated—potentially—for 24 h per day, seven days a week.

[6] A good analogy is the drive technology in electric automobiles that has dispensed with the traditional drive technology of internal combustion engines (transmission, drive shaft, differential, axles).

Report of the Committee on Recent Economic Changes: Estimates of Conversion to EUD

Unfortunately, the role of acceleration and machine speed in driving productivity growth was poorly understood in the 1920s. Production theory at the time (as well as now) was devoid of energy, let alone machine speed. However, several perspicacious references can be found in the timely report of President Herbert Hoover's *Committee of Recent Economic Changes* where there is an overwhelming emphasis placed on power in general and on electric unit drive in particular. Chapter after chapter, section after section, author after author makes reference to the increasing use of electric power as the driving force behind the exceptional growth in the 1920s. Here are excerpts taken from the three chapters that dealt specifically with the new technology—specifically, electric unit drive.

> *Section 1 – Characteristics of the Years 1922-1929*
> *Invention is not a new art........But the breadth and scale and "tempo" of recent developments given them new importance.*
> *The increased supply of power and its wider uses; the multiplication by man of his strength and skill through machinery.*
> *The Speed Which Power Has Added to Production*
> *Characteristic also has been the rise and use of power – three and three-quarters times faster than the growth in population – and the extent to which power has been made readily available not alone for driving tools of increasing size and capacity, but for a convenient diversity of purposes in the smallest business enterprise and on the farm and the home. P. xi*

Part 2-Technical Changes in Manufacturing Industries, L. P. Alford

> *In a preceding part of this report, it has been shown that the increasing primary power available to each worker in manufacturing establishments is one of the most important and significant changes which have taken place since* 1919. *This not the only significant change to power utilization. There have been increases in the installation of electric motors to supply mechanical power in manufacturing in the amount of power purchased instead of generated by manufacturing establishments, in the efficiency of prime movers. The first of these trends account, in part, for the rapid development of electric public utility companies. The increase in the capacity of prime movers which supply power to manufacturing establishments is a rough measure of the increased use of machinery by those establishments.*

Increase in Electric Motor Power.-The electric motor first appeared as a factor in industrial power in 1899, the amount of power purchased at the time and applied through electric motors being but 1.8 percent. So rapid has been the increase, however, that in 1927, the last year for which we have statistics, nearly 50 percent of the power applied in manufacture was by means of electric motors operating on purchased power. P. 126
Part 3-The Changing Structure of Industry, Willard L. Thorp
Scale of Production in Terms of Horse Power. – The record for horse power per establishment offers a much clearer picture of growth. The census figures refer to the total rated horse-power capacity of engines, motors, and other prime movers. Motors run by power generated within the establishment are excluded as involving duplication, since the power producer which runs the generator is already included. Because the figures refer to total rated capacity, they are considerably larger than if they were the amount of power in actual daily use.
As one might expect the range of power capacity among the industries is tremendous. The hairwork industry, with 87 establishments, reports but 13 horse power in total, or less than 0.15 per establishment. At the other extreme is the copper smelting industry with 26 establishments and a total of 326,509 horse power per establishment.
The average values for the industries emphasize the steadiness and degree of the advance. That this tendency is general is indicated by the fact that in 1925, five-sixths of the industries showed increased horse- power over 1914.
If one keeps in mind the fact that horse power is gaining on average much more than wage earners, Table 8 can be accepted as a clear demonstration of the interrelation between the two devices which have been used to measure size. There are cases where horse power is gaining and wage earners are declining. P. 179

Alternating Current (AC) and the Emergence of Large-Scale Utilities

While EUD held out great promise in so far as power drive technologies were concerned, it had one important disadvantage, namely, the power source. In the early years, converting from steam-powered belting and shafting to EUD required an on-site power plant, complete with an extensive in-house distribution network delivering power throughout the plant. The cost, including the dismantling of the cumbersome shafting and belting equipment in place, was oftentimes prohibitive—at least before its expected lifetime (i.e., 20 years).

As it turned out, a number of developments in the 1910s would change all of this, making EUD the preferred power drive technology. These included the development of AC power, which could be transmitted over long distances, the development of large-scale electrical utilities, and grid interconnection. All three combined to not only lower the cost of power, but to make it available literally wherever and whenever it was needed. Companies no longer had to invest in generating and transmitting power. Instead, they could concentrate on the tasks at hand, namely, producing.

This section describes these developments and their impact on material processes, the most important of which was acceleration. Unshackled from the physical limits of belting and shafting, process speeds increased throughout this period, thus increasing productivity. In short, with the same tools and supervision (labor), more could be produced per period of time. Einstein referred to this as improved techniques.

Alternating Current Versus Direct Current

The development of three-phase alternating current (AC) was a key development in the electric power revolution. Direct current (DC) had the unfortunate disadvantage of not being transmissible beyond a certain distance, beyond which it would lose much of its force. This made for a situation in which the power had to be generated at or near the point of use/consumption. Put differently, companies had to generate DC electricity on site.

All of this changed with the development of three-phase alternating current by Nikolai Tesla and George Westinghouse. Now, electricity could be produced and distributed over long distances. Transmission losses were minimal in comparison to direct current. Large-scale power-generation plants could now be built. Extensive distribution networks could now be built. Companies could now purchase electric power at a fraction of the cost of generating it. More importantly, these same companies could now distribute power throughout their plants with little-to-no loss—compared to the highly inefficient and cumbersome belting and shafting of yore.

Large-Scale Electrical Utilities

The introduction of AC current payed the way for the development of large-scale power utilities. In the early years, most were thermal power-generating stations, consuming fossil fuels—mostly coal. However, with time, hydraulic power-generating stations entered the fray. Turbines that had up until then powered belting and shafting were converted to AC electric power-generating stations.

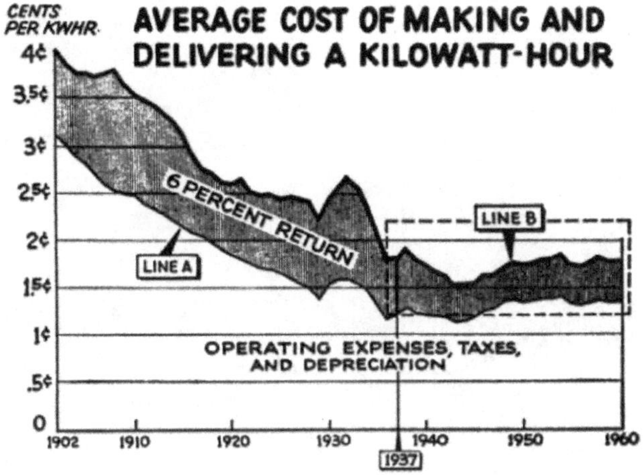

Fig. 5.3 Average cost of generating and delivering a kWh

Throughout this period, the cost of electric power, measured in kWhs, decreased monotonically. Substantial economies of scale resulted in monotonically decreasing costs (and prices) for kWhs (see Fig. 5.3).

Part III War Industries Board and the Push for Mass Production

Interconnection

The second key development/innovation in this period was grid interconnection, by which it should be understood, the pooling of the local power grids in the form of networks. Given important variations in the demand for power across users and across time, interconnection offered the possibility of offering power on an integrated grid, where nonsynchronous users could make use of the power, oftentimes at a discount. The end result was a massive increase in power availability and a marked decrease in price, the latter owing to the reduced cost of operating thermal plants on a continuous basis, as opposed to an on/off basis (Figs. 5.4 and 5.5).

Interconnectivity: The Role of the War Industries Board

A key impetus in the drive to interconnectivity was the War Industries Board (WIB) created by President Woodrow Wilson in 1918, the purpose of which was to increase America's capacity to produce armaments in

Fig. 5.4 Conowingo and Wilson hydroelectric dams

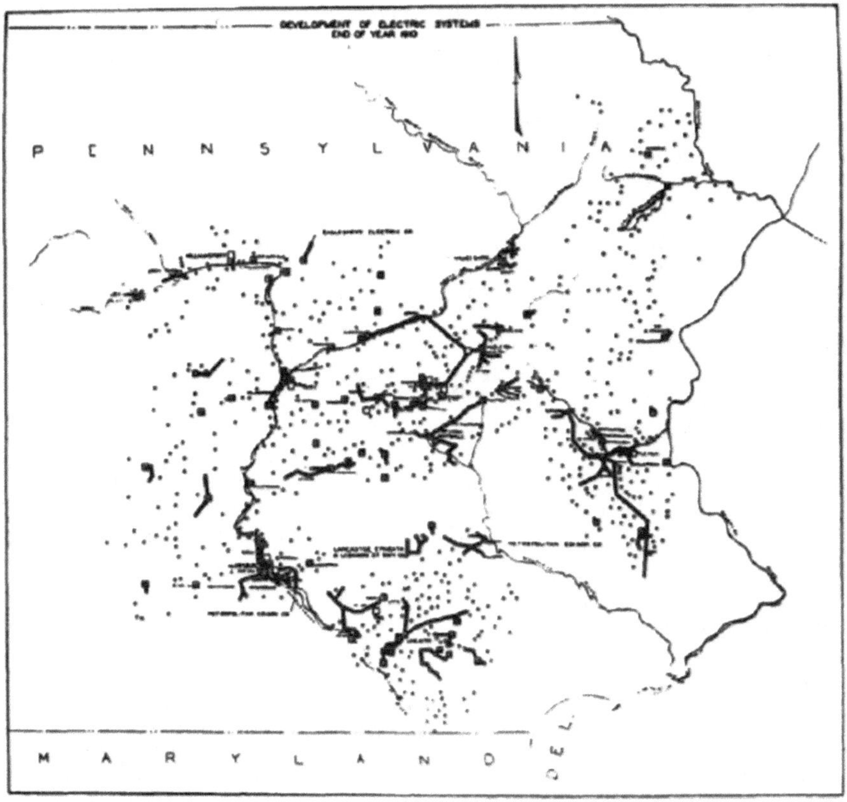

Fig. 5.5 Electrical utility interconnection, Pennsylvania, 1920

wartime. By the 1910s, a key input in the production of armaments was nitrogen (for explosives). A new process for extracting/fixing this element from atmospheric oxygen had been developed in Germany (known as the Haber-Bosch process), a process that required abundant supplies of energy (see Table 5.3).

Because the US production of nitrogen, a key input in the armament industry, had fallen behind that of Germany, the WIB recommended the creation, by the government, of a plant in Sterling, Georgia, with the express purpose of closing the gap. The corresponding electric power would be supplied ultimately by the development of the Muscle Shoals river basin and by increasing interconnectivity. In other words, parochial

Table 5.3 Electricity generated, 1912–1930 (million kWhs)

Year	*Total utilities and industrial establishments*	*Utilities*	*Industrial establishments*	*Hydro*	*Steam and internal combustion*
1912	24,752	11,569	13,183	7337	17,365
1917	43,427	25,438	17,991	13,948	29,481
1920	56,559	39,405	17,154	20,311	36,248
1921	53,125	37,180	15,945	18,732	34,393
1922	61,204	43,632	17,572	21,262	39,942
1923	71,399	51,229	20,170	23,421	47,978
1924	75,892	54,662	21,230	24,138	51,754
1925	84,666	61,451	23,215	26,112	58,554
1926	94,222	69,353	24,869	30,355	63,867
1927	101,390	75,418	25,972	32,924	68,466
1928	108,069	82,794	25,275	37,297	70,772
1929	116,747	92,180	24,567	37,038	79,709
1930	114,637	91,112	23,525	34,874	79,768

Source: US Department of Commerce (1975), Historical Statistics of the United States, S-32-43

interests would be sacrificed for the national good. According to Hughes (1983)

> *The technology of electric power systems that was introduced during World War I not only caused perturbations in trends but also carried into peacetime certain aspects of the wartime environment. The extremely large electric generating stations that were built to fill the pressing and unusual needs for electric power during World War I survived the war and became, in a sense, a solution in search of a problem. Another, less obvious case, is the large number of interconnections of electric light and power systems that were made during the emergencies of wartime and carried over into peacetime. P. 286*

The Evidence
Power Generation and Interconnectivity as Seen by Herbert Hoover's Committee on Recent Economic Changes

President Herbert Hoover's *Committee on Recent Economic Changes* was unequivocal: Innovations in power use and generation were the driving force behind the astonishing growth of the 1920s. Regarding the power generation, it pointed out:

The growth of the size of central station machinery should be noted. The first large turbo-generator built by General Electric Co. about 1900 was of 5,000-kilowatt capacity. Today, single units of 50,000 kilowatt are common, combined units of 100,000 kilowatt not unusual and one of 208,000-kilowatt capacity is under construction. The new State Line Power House of the Chicago Edison Co. will have a final capacity of 1,000,000 kilowatts, and there is no apparent diminution to the growth of such plants, either as to size or number. A survey of our public utilities in the Blakemore Analytic Reports, dated December 20, 1926, gives the total horse power of prime movers in this industry as 3,000,000 in 1902; 12,000,000 in 1912, 24,000,000 in 1922 and a prospective 30,000,000 in 1930. P. 91

From the beginnings of the Industrial Revolution to the early twentieth century, the power to drive industrial processes was generated on-site and transmitted to the various work processes within the plant using shafting and belting technology. Coal and coke were used to fuel successive generations of boilers which produced steam to drive what was, in most cases, a single Boulton-Watt steam engine, which, in turn, powered belts and shafts and, ultimately, the myriad tools of the Industrial Revolution, whether directly via a central shaft or via a DC generator that powered a single DC motor that powered the belts and shafts. All this would change in the 1910s and 1920s owing, in large measure, to the emergence of (i) large-scale electricity generating plants and (ii) interconnectivity or, put simply, electrical grids. In this section, we examine this important development. Companies which had, until then, generated their own power, whether in the form of steam or steam-generated DC electricity, converted to electric unit drive powered by inexpensive publicly or privately provided electricity. Less cumbersome than shafting and belting, capital costs decreased. More importantly, process speeds increased, thus increasing productivity.

The emergence of large-scale utilities in the 1910s and 1920s was the result of a number of factors, the most important of which was World War I and its exigencies. WWI witnessed the bringing on-stream of 27,836 million utility-generated kWwhs, thus tripling output.[7] More importantly, it showcased the possibility and value of these large-scale undertakings, especially in regard to providing abundant and affordable power.

[7] Utility-generated capacity stood at 11,569 million kWhs in 1912 and 39,405 million kWhs in 1920. Source: US Department of Commerce (1975). Series S-32-43.

The War Industries Board

Perhaps the most important impetus to the widespread conversion of US industry to electric unit drive was the War Industries Board of 1917, created by executive order with the mandate to oversee government procurement of war supplies. More specifically, it was to: "coordinate the purchase of war supplies between the War Department (Department of the Army) and the Navy Department. Because the United States Department of Defense (The Pentagon) would only come into existence in 1947, this was an ad hoc construction to promote cooperation between the Army and the Navy (with regard to procurement), it was founded by the Council of National Defense (which on its turn came into existence by the appropriation bill of August 1916)." In addition to coordinating the purchase of war supplies, it was also active on a number of policy fronts, notably in (i) encouraging US industry to adopt the mass production techniques made famous by the Ford Motor Company and (ii) investing heavily in the nitrate and cyanamide industries (National Defense Act of 1916). The latter would employ the newly developed Haber-Bosch process which was energy intensive, specifically electricity-intensive. A nitrate plant was built in Sheffield, Alabama, and a cyanamide plant in Muscle Shoals. To supply power to the latter, a hydroelectric station and dam were to be completed at Muscle Shoals.

Throughout its brief history, the War Industries Board openly promoted the construction of large-scale electricity-generating plants, in part to power the various war-related industries. This had the effect of increasing the availability of relatively cheap electric power, which, in turn, accelerated the conversion to electric unit drive. Formally, it acted on both the demand and supply sides of the market, increasing the demand for war supplies and openly encouraging firms to increase supply.

Summary and Conclusions

Despite being at the underlying cause of the First and Second Industrial Revolutions, and indeed, of the manifold increases in wealth that have characterized the entire industrial era, power drive technology and innovations to these technologies have been a largely forgotten element in production theory. References to the steam engine and the electric motor notwithstanding, the role of power in wealth and growth has been largely ignored. This is somewhat surprising given the role of energy in the physics (classical mechanics, kinetics, and thermodynamics) of material processes in general (i.e., those outside of economics).

This chapter focused on power drive technologies in general and electric unit drive, in particular, the latter being the key element that increased the potential rated capacity of the US industry throughout the 1920s and 1930s, thus being the prime source of the Roaring Twenties.

A number of things stand out, not the least of which is the invisible, stealth-like nature of electric unit drive–based acceleration. Machine speed-ups are largely imperceptible to even the seasoned observer. After all, the only thing that will have changed is the speed at which given material processes operate. This explains in part both the dearth of work and writing on it, as well as the difficulty scholars had in describing the changes in the 1920s, referring to it cryptically as velocity. That machine speeds were not and are not a part of production theory either in engineering or economics goes a long way to explain this oversight.

Nonetheless, the fact of the matter is that machine/process speeds were increasing throughout the 1920s, increasing conventionally defined productivity and vastly increasing the rated capacity of existing labor and capital. As Alfred D. Chandler pointed out

> *In modern mass production, as in modern mass distribution and modern transportation and communications, economies resulted more from speed than from size. It was not the size of the manufacturing establishment in terms of the number of workers and the amount and value of productive equipment, but the velocity of throughput and the resulting increase in volume that permitted economies that lowered costs and increased output per worker and per machine. (Chandler,* 1977, *p. 244)*

Just how these changes would affect productivity and output is the subject of the next chapter. How companies would respond to these changes is the subject of the subsequent chapter. Taken together, these two chapters provide a detailed analysis of what Einstein referred to as "improvements in technique and organization" and their effects on the demand for what he referred to as "labor-power"—conventional labor.

References

Beaudreau, B. C. (1998). *Energy and organization: Growth and distribution Reexamined*. Greenwood Press.

Beaudreau, B. C. (2020). *The economics of speed: Machine speed as the key factor in productivity*. Springer.

Chandler, A. D. (1977). *The visible hand: The managerial revolution in American business*. Harvard University Press.

Devine, W. D., Jr. (1983). From shafts to wires: Historical perspective on electrification. *The Journal of Economic History, 43*, 347–372.

Devine, W. D., Jr. (1990). Electrified mechanical drive: The historical power distribution revolution. In S. H. Schurr, C. C. Burwell, W. D. Devine Jr., & S. Sonenblum (Eds.), *Electricity in the American Economy: Agent of technological Progress*. Greenwood Press.

Hughes, T. P. (1983). *Networks of power: Electrification in Western society 1880–1930*. The Johns Hopkins University Press.

Rosenberg, N. (1972). *Technology and American economic growth*. M.E. Sharpe.

Sonenblum, S. (1990). Electrification and productivity growth in manufacturing. In S. H. Schurr, C. C. Burwell, W. D. Devine Jr., & S. Sonenblum (Eds.), *Electricity in the American Economy: Agent of technological Progress*. Greenwood Press.

U.S. Department of Commerce. (1975). *Historical statistics of the United States, colonial times to 1970*. U.S. Government Printing Office.

CHAPTER 6

Machine Speed, Acceleration, and Rated Capacity in the 1920s: The Evidence

Abstract This chapter provides a series of estimates of US potential GDP in the 1920s and 1930s drawn from myriad sources. Acceleration increased potential GDP by increasing the rated capacity of existing as well as new plants. Among the studies presented are surveys of the nation's managers conducted by the Brookings Institution. Indirect estimates are also provided based on productivity, wage, and stock market data.

Keywords US GDP • Potential GDP • Rated capacity • Productivity

> *Our transportation systems, our industrial processes, our factory machinery—all these have felt the magic hand of speed—controlled speed that has given us more things to enjoy and more time in which to enjoy them: that has produced more goods for more people at less cost and that has created a better standard of living for the average man. These are the benefits of ever-increasing speed and accurate control.*
> *(General Electric Company, 1937)*

Introduction

Acceleration and speed defined the 1920s. The hum of the dynamos gave us the roar of the twenties, the proverbial Roaring Twenties. Charlie Chaplin immortalized the place of speed in what has since become known

B. C. Beaudreau, *Energy, Einstein, and the Great Depression*,
https://doi.org/10.1007/978-3-032-26664-4_6

as the Second Industrial Revolution in his 1936 classic *Modern Times*, where speed, specifically greater and greater machine speeds, is the chief protagonist in the story. In what is the defining moment of the movie, the CEO of the Electro-Steel company instructs a bare-chested employee to increase the operating speed of processes and sub-processes throughout the plant, leading to the emotional and physical breakdown of the main character, played by Chaplin himself.

Just how greater and greater machine speeds affected productivity was and remains poorly understood, analytically speaking. It could be argued that its nonmaterial nature constituted the chief obstacle in identifying it.[1] It could, however, be argued that Albert Einstein, being the most celebrated physicist of his era, should have picked up on this. After all, understanding the mechanics and kinetics of material processes would have been a trivial exercise for someone of his stature. But alas, it wasn't to be. At best, he, like many others, felt that something had changed, something he referred to as "technical progress."

In this chapter, evidence of the acceleration-based increase in productivity and potential output in the 1920s is presented. To begin with, it is important to point out that owing to the nature of the new drive technology, there are no actual data on potential output/rated capacity at the firm-, industry-, or economy-wide level for the 1920s and 1930s. Acceleration increases the potential rated capacity of existing capital without necessarily increasing actual output. Second, the diffusion of EUD was not generalized throughout the USA nor instantaneous. In fact, parts of the service sector were not affected—specifically, those that were not based on inanimate energy. Not all firms within a given industry adopted the new technology in the 1920s. In fact, the evidence shows that the conversion to EUD occurred throughout the 1920s and 1930s. The estimates presented here consist of a combination of survey results as well as indirect measures of overall productivity growth based on conventional measures, such as reported labor productivity (see Table 6.1).

[1] For example, a photo of a car traveling at 30 mph will be identical to a photo of that same car traveling at 60 mph. Yet the latter will be twice as productive as the former.

Table 6.1 Pre-crash excess capacity as seen in the literature

Howard Scott et al. (1933)	The United States of our forefathers, with 12,000,000 inhabitants, performed its necessary work in almost entire dependence upon the human engine, which, as its chief means of energy conversion, was aided and abetted only by domestic animals and a few water wheels. The United States today has over one billion installed hp. In 1929, these engines of energy conversion, though operated only to partial capacity, nevertheless, had an output that represented approximately 50% of the total work of the world. (Scott et al., 1933, p. 54)
Paul Douglas (1927)	The second factor which has contributed to our prosperity has been our development of automatic and efficient machinery and of effective technical processes. (Douglas, 1927, p. 26)
Irving Fisher (1930)	"acceleration rather than structural change is the key to an understanding of our recent economic developments." (Fisher, 1930, p. 3) "But the breadth and the tempo of recent developments gives them new importance."
Rexford Tugwell (1927)	"revolution underway in U.S. industry." Foremost among the "technical causes" of increased productivity, he argued, was "the bringing into use of new and better power resources more suited to our technique, more flexible and less wasteful; and continued progress in the technique of generating and applying power" (Tugwell, 1927, p. 180)
Stuart Chase (1934)	A point at which consumption becomes a greater problem than production. Circa 1920. "Our economy," says F.L. Ackerman, "is so set up that it produces goods at a higher rate than it produces income with which to purchase them."(Chase, 1934, p. 11)
Harold Loeb (1935)	"The budget total $135,516,000,000, an increase of some $43 billion, over the actual production of 1929. The goods and services represented by this consist of desired goods and services which the people of the United States could produce but do not produce." (Loeb, 1935, p. 238)

Estimates of Output Gap/Definition of Rated Capacity

Throughout the 1920s, there were numerous references to the purported widening gap between potential and actual output. Few, however, provided actual estimates. Was potential output 20%, 30%, or 40% greater than actual output? By how much had EUD increased firms' ability to produce? Only a decade later, in the depths of the depression, would estimates of the excess capacity be published, first by the Brookings Institution and then by Harold Loeb and the New York Housing Authority.

Table 6.2 The Brookings Institution estimates of excess productive capacity, 1922–1929

Year	*Potential productive capacity*	*Actual GDP*	*Gap (%)*
1922	75.5	63.4	16
1923	83.2	69.9	17
1924	85.1	71.5	17
1925	89.6	75.3	16
1926	91.9	77.2	16
1927	93.2	78.3	17
1928	94.9	79.7	16
1929	97.5	81.9	17

Source: Nourse (1934), p. 176

The Brookings Institution

The first set of estimates of generalized excess capacity in the US economy in the 1920s was provided by the Brookings Institution, founded and headed by Robert S. Brookings.[2] In what has to be described as an extremely ambitious project, it set out in the early 1930s to estimate what it referred to as "America's Ability to Produce." As potential output is just that, a potential, an extensive survey of the nation's manufacturers was conducted. More specifically, a survey targeting production managers focused on obtaining estimates of the company's potential as opposed to actual output. Put simply, they were asked to estimate potential output, whether or not they had ever produced at that level. The results were reported in a series of volumes in the mid-1930s. Table 6.2, taken from "America's Ability to Produce," reports an output gap of 16–17%. It is important to understand that these are estimates of potential output. Actual values may be either higher or lower.

Harold Loeb (1935)

A similar attempt was made by Harold Loeb and the New York Housing Authority in 1935. In a report entitled "The Chart of Plenty: A Study on America's Product Capacity Based on the Finding of the National Survey

[2] Robert S. Brookings was a successful businessman who took an active interest in the affairs of the nation, specifically in the gap between the nation's ability to produce and its actual level of wealth. The bulk of his thinking on this matter can be found in his 1932 book, Brookings, *The Way Forward* published by the MacMillan Co.

Table 6.3 Statement of losses to the American people (billions of 1929 dollars)

Year	*Budget*	*National income*	*Actual loss to consumer*
1929	135	93	42
1930	137	86	51
1931	138	79	59
1932	139	69	70
1933	141	76	65
Total loss to consumer (1929–1933)			287

Source: Loeb (1935)

of Potential Product Capacity," he and his associates provided estimates of excess capacity based on survey data. The gist of both the study and its findings can be found in the following quote:

> *Practicability of Capacity Production. It might be contended that higher speeds of operation would lead to breakdowns of both plant and personnel. Fifty years ago, this might have been true. Then, most of the labor was purely physical, of a repetitive nature, hard on the worker and destructive of his morale and well-being. Today, as industrial electrification has progressed, controls are becoming simple, a matter of push-button manipulation and entirely automatic; and labor, when it is not carried out along primitive lines such as digging, plastering and similar operations, has in many cases assumed a supervisory character. As a result, the attainment of higher speeds of output does not wear out the labor force as it once did. (Loeb,* 1935, *p. xxiii).*

The upshot of the report is summarized in Table 6.3, where, according to the study, potential GDP in 1929 was 42% greater than the actual output of 93 billion. This gap would, over the subsequent years, reach 70% in 1932, the depth of the downturn. The cumulative loss of wealth to the nation was 287 billion over this five-year period. Table 6.4 presents the report's estimates of physical productivity per worker from 1870 to 1930.

The lead author and instigator of the project was Harold Loeb, a New York City writer, someone with no training or experience in economics, business, engineering, or other related fields.[3] That this was the case

[3] Harold Albert Loeb (October 18, 1891–January 20, 1974) was an American writer, notable as an important American figure in the arts among expatriates in Paris in the 1920s. In 1921, he was the founding editor of Broom, an international literary and art magazine, which was first published in New York City before he moved the venture to Europe. Loeb published two novels while living in Paris in the 1920s and additional works after returning to New York in 1929.

Table 6.4 Physical productivity (efficiency) per worker by census periods 1870–1930 (1900 productivity = 100)

Census year	*Agriculture*	*Manufacturing*	*Mining*
1870	58	64	36
1880	77	75	56
1890	82	93	84
1900	100	100	100
1910	100	117	104
1920	119	131	139
1930	141	163	147

speaks to the general mood of the period in question, a mood that Einstein had also dialed into. In short, there appeared to be a consensus, running across virtually all professions, all fields, and all classes, that "technical progress" had created unprecedented potential in so far as the country's ability to create wealth.

Backward Induction-Based Estimates

Beaudreau (1996) estimated potential output in the 1920s using basic growth theory—a technique known as backward extrapolation. According to standard growth theory, gross domestic product grows at rate $n + \tau$, where n is the rate of labor force growth and τ is the rate of technological change—in this case, the percentage rate of acceleration-based productivity growth. Since acceleration does not necessarily translate instantaneously into output growth, actual GNP data will fail to capture potential output. To get around this, backward extrapolation techniques proceed by making the strong assumption that they will, over time, work themselves into the growth rate and, hence, into actual GDP. By identifying that point in time, estimates of potential GDP for the preceding years can be obtained by extrapolating actual GDP for the year in question back in time at the rate of growth of the labor supply.

For example, suppose that the US economy was producing at its potential in 1944. That is, by 1944, in the depth of World War II, companies throughout the US economy were producing at their new, accelerated, higher rated capacity. Potential GDP for the years prior to 1944 can then be estimated by simply discounting 1944 actual GDP by the rate of growth of the labor force—that is, the rate at which the economy would grow in

Table 6.5 Backward extrapolation estimates of potential US gross domestic product

Base year (t')/Target year (t")[1]	*1925*	*1927*	*1929*
1943	242.3[2]	251.4	260.7
	(0.3508)[3]	(0.3245)	(0.2809)
1944	255.0	264.5	274.4
	(0.4216)	(0.3938)	(0.3164)

[1] Base and target years are reversed owing to the nature of the corresponding estimates (i.e., backward-looking)

[2] Actual US GDP/(I+0.0185)[18]

[3] Potential US GDP/Actual GDP-1 (billion constant 1958 dollars)

the absence of technological change. In 1944, US GDP stood at $361.3 billion. The rate of growth of the US nonagricultural labor force from 1910 to 1950 was estimated at 1.85% per annum. Potential 1925 GDP, it therefore follows, can be obtained by dividing $361.3 billion by 1.4166404 (i.e., (1.0185)19), the appropriate discount factor, which yields $255.0 billion. Dividing the former by the level of actual 1925 US GDP of $179.4 billion yields a value for an EUD-based productivity growth of 0.4216. That is, the resulting estimate of τ, the EUD-based technology shock, in this case, is 42.1%.

The first set of estimates of potential US GDP and resulting values for τ, the technology shock, is presented in Table 6.5. Two base years (i.e., t'), 1944 and 1943, and three target years (i.e., t''), 1925, 1927, and 1929, were chosen. In 1943, real US GDP was $337.1 billion (constant 1958 dollars), which, extrapolated backward to 1925 at an annual rate of 1.85%, yields a value for potential US GDP in 1925 of $242.3 billion (see Fig. 6.1). That is, the actual 1925 US GDP of $242.3 billion, growing at an annual rate of 1.85%, the rate of growth of the labor force over this period, yields a level of 1943 US GDP of $337.1 billion. Dividing this figure by the reported actual 1925 GDP of $179.4 billion (constant 1958 dollars) yields a value for τ, the rate of technological change, of 0.3508 (reported in parentheses). By choosing 1944 as the relevant base year, potential 1925 US GDP increases to $255.3 billion, which corresponds to a value for τ of 0.4216.

Thus, potential US GDP, as defined by EUD-based accelerated speed in 1925 (i.e., mass production), was between 35 (t' = 1943) and 42 (t' = 1944) percent greater than actual GDP (see Fig. 6.1). Similarly,

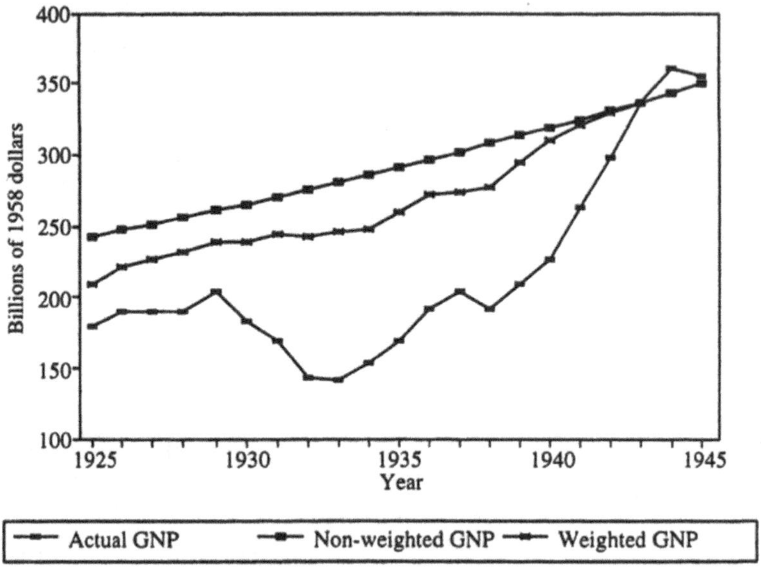

Fig. 6.1 Actual and potential US gross domestic product, 1925–1945 (weighted and unweighted). Source: US Department of Commerce (1975), series F47

potential US GDP in 1927 was between 23 (t' = 1943) and 39 (t' = 1944) percent greater than actual GDP, and lastly, potential GNP in 1929 was between 23 (t' = 1943) and 34 (t' = 1944) percent greater than actual GNP.

Productivity-Based Estimates of τ

The logic of backward extrapolation can also be used to estimate aggregate and sector-specific values for τ: from reported labor productivity data for the base and target years. In this case, it is assumed that EUD-based acceleration affected both labor and capital productivity. As a result, estimates of τ were obtained by simply differencing labor productivity at times t' and t''.

The resulting set of estimates of τ for t'' = 1924, 1925, and 1926, based on labor productivity growth data from 1924 to 1944, is provided in Table 6.6, where values range from 80.3% (end-of-base year 1923 to end-of-target year 1944) to 58.9% (end-of-base year 1925 to end-of-target

Table 6.6 Labor productivity–based estimates of τ

Target year (t')/ Base year (t")[1]	*Total*[2] *1924*	*Man. 1924*	*Total 1925*	*Man. 1925*	*Total 1926*	*Man. 1926*
1926	7.03	15.67	2.46	8.84	2.69	1.97
1928	8.89	23.63	4.26	16.12	4.49	8.99
1930	9.60	30.39	4.93	22.19	5.16	14.69
1932	6.32	25.62	1.79	17.99	2.02	10.74
1934	14.75	42.78	9.86	23.44	10.11	25.87
1936	24.59	53.23	19.28	43.92	19.55	35.08
1938	28.10	49.00	22.64	39.95	22.92	31.35
1940	37.00	70.89	31.16	61.51	31.46	50.65
1942	45.19	80.09	39.01	69.15	39.32	58.77
1944	57.37	80.34	50.67	69.39	51.01	58.99

The price level (1958=100) increased from 51.3 in 1923 to 58.2 in 1944

Source: US Department of Commerce (1975), Series D86 and D685

[1] End-of-year data

[2] (Output per man-hour in t'-output per man-hour in *t*")/(output per man-hour in *t*")

year 1944). For the US economy as a whole, they range from 57.3% (1924–1944) to 51.0% (1926–1944).

Stock Market–Based Estimates of the Technology Shock

If individuals from all walks of life felt that something fundamental had changed, there is every reason to believe that the stock market, in general, and fully informed investors, in particular, would not only have been "in the loop," so to speak, but also would have acted on this information, bidding up the price of stocks.

In this section, estimates of EUD-based technical progress are inferred from stock price movements before the 1929 stock market crash. To begin, consider the relationship between EUD-based acceleration and expected earnings/dividends. As there are no scientific or historical grounds (i.e., labor productivity per se) for wages to increase, this raises an important question: How do investors, in general, and investors in the 1920s, in particular, see the relationship between technological change—in this case, EUD - and real wages? More to the point, when estimating the earnings potential of the introduction of a new technology, do they factor in wage increases? Or do they simply assume that wages will remain where they are?

Admittedly, this is an empirical question. For investors to factor in anticipated wage increases, it would have to be the case that in the past, output-increasing process innovations like EUD-based acceleration systematically led to higher wages; otherwise, there would be no reason to believe that they would do so. On this note, the empirical evidence shows the absence of a one-to-one relationship between real wages and productivity. It would therefore not be unreasonable to assume that investors in the late 1920s played what amounted to a Nash strategy vis-à-vis wages.

This has important implications for expected dividends and, hence, for stock prices. For example, it implies that since the proportion of earnings constitutes a fraction (i.e., roughly 30%) of total firm income, expected dividends from EUD-based acceleration would increase by more than τ%. In fact, they would increase by a multiple of τ. Consider the following numerical example. Let α define the ratio of capital income to total firm income and suppose that $r = 0.3$. Hypothetical total firm revenue of $100 would yield factor payments to capital on the order of $30, which, capitalized at a rate of interest of 3% per annum, would yield a stock value of $1000. Now, assume that τ takes on a value of 0.40. That is, EUD-based acceleration increases productivity by 40%. For a constant nominal wage and assuming that the firm is not constrained in product markets, the resulting stock value would rise to $2333, as the anticipated $40 rise in earnings would be factored entirely into the stock price. The rate at which the hypothetical stock price would rise is given as τ/r, which in this case is 1.33 (133%). Thus, a 40% increase in the stock price is magnified by a factor of 3.325.

This technique was used to estimate τ_s, τ_m, τ_r, and τ_u, the implicit-in-stock price technology shock in the economy as a whole, manufacturing (industrials), railroads, and utilities, respectively, using Standard and Poor's indices of stock market prices from 1923 to 1929. Referring to Table 6.7, real share prices for total, industrial, railroad, and utilities increased 238%, 231%, 102%, and 230%, respectively, from 1924 to 1929. This implies that by 1929, the initial hypothetical book value of $1000 in each of these sectors would have risen to $3380 for the market as a whole, $3310 for manufacturing, $2020 for railroads, and $3300 for utilities. For these prices to exist in financial market equilibria, anticipated sector earnings of $101.40, $99.30, $60.60, and $99.00 are required, which, when

Table 6.7 Stock market–based estimates of τ, 1924–1929

Stock index	*1929*	*1923*	*Growth*	τ
1924–1929				
Total S&P	56.42	16.71	238	71
Industrials S&P	42.19	12.74	231	69
Industrials DJIA	352.51	95.52	269	81
Railroads S&P	91.27	45.13	102	31
Utilities S&P	117.25	35.30	230	69
1925–1929				
Total S&P	51.42	17.67	191	57
Industrials S&P	42.19	13.34	216	65
Industrials DJIA	352.51	120.51	192	57
Railroads S&P	91.27	48.86	87	26
Utilities S&P	117.25	37.79	210	63
1926–1929				
Total S&P	51.42	21.48	139	42
Industrials S&P	42.19	16.74	152	46
Industrials DJIA	352.51	156.66	125	37
Railroads S&P	91.27	57.63	76	23
Utilities S&P	117.25	45.05	160	48

Source: US Department of Commerce (1975), series X-487-491; Pierce (1991)

initial earnings of $30.00 are netted out, yield values for τ_s, τ_m, τ_r, and τ_u, of 71%, 69%, 31%, and 69%, respectively.

The way to interpret these results is as follows. Hypothetical, fully informed investors knowing that τ_s, τ_m, τ_r, and τ_u stood at 71%, 69%, 31%, and 69%, respectively, would have bid up the value of market, industrial, railroad, and utility shares by 238%, 231%, 102%, and 230%, respectively.[4] In other words, changing fundamentals would have led investors to bid share prices up by 238%, 231%, 102%, and 230%, respectively. What is particularly noteworthy is the fact that the greatest gains occurred in those sectors most likely to be affected by electric power and EUD, notably industry and utilities.

[4] These estimates assume that all of the resulting greater income would accrue to capital.

Income and Expenditure Inertia: Evidence

Income and expenditure inertia will, according to the model presented above, manifest itself in $h(t)$, the average number of hours worked per day, itself a measure of capacity utilization. According to Eq. 4.1, an increase in $s(t)$, average machine/process speed, will, ceteris paribus, create a disequilibrium between potential output, on the one hand, and actual income and expenditure, on the other, resulting in a decrease in $h(t)$ as firms adjust to the new higher per-hour productivity. This owes to two factors, namely, the fact that wages are fixed and profits (payments to capital), being a residual form of factor remuneration, remain constant.

Greater machine/process speeds increase output per hour worked. However, because labor is not the source of the increase, there is no reason to believe that companies will increase—or be inclined to increase—wages. The second factor has to do with the fact that, unlike labor, capital is not remunerated prior to the sale of the product/output, but rather is remunerated after. Another way of looking at this is that the owners of capital (i.e., investors) are, as University of Chicago economics professor Frank Knight pointed out in 1921, residual claimants (Knight, 1921). Together, these two factors make for income and consequently expenditure inertia in the face of greater rated capacity.

This creates a situation of income and expenditure inertia in which actual national income is less than potential output, as defined by potential rated capacity, making for expenditure levels that are also less than potential output. Put differently, income and expenditure are less than the level of full employment income. In such a setting, the only possible way out would consist of price (excluding wages) deflation, which, in turn, would prompt an increase in real wages and an equivalent increase in real profits. As a result, the productivity gains from acceleration would be shared between the two factor inputs. There is, however, reason to believe that companies would resist such price decreases in the short run, preferring to adjust $h(t)$, a phenomenon Thorstein Veblen referred to as "sabotage." Part of the reason owes to the fact that there was no guarantee that others would do likewise and that overall demand would increase proportionately.

It is important to understand the differences between this view and the classic underconsumption view found in the literature, which maintains that a weak marginal propensity to consume reduces overall expenditure, therefore decreasing output and employment. Here, the lack of consumption owes to what we refer to as underincome or income inertia, which, by definition, implies underconsumption. Firms choose not to produce at capacity for lack of sufficient demand.

Income Inertia as Seen by President Hoover's Committee on Recent Economic Changes

As it turned out, this disequilibrium and response were at the core of the report of President Herbert Hoover's *Committee on Recent Economic Changes*, published in 1929. After having extolled the virtues of electric power, the committee focused on what it viewed as the overriding problem, namely, the lack of balance, by which it should be understood, the balance between the US's ability to produce wealth and its ability to consume it. In short, it held that the two were increasingly out of balance, with the former exceeding the latter.

> *In the marked balance of consumption and production, for example, the control of the economic organism is increasingly evident. With the development of a stream of credit to facilitate business operations, and with flexible power to energize industry and to increase the effectiveness of the workers, has come an increasing evenness in the flow of production.*
>
> *Once an intermittent starting and stopping of production-consumption was characteristic of the economic situation. It was jerky and unpredictable, and overproduction was followed by a pause for consumption to catch up. For the seven years under survey, a more marked balance of production-consumption is evident.*
>
> *Our complex and intricate economic machine can produce, but to keep it producing continuously it must be maintained in balance*

Income Inertia and Unemployment: The Case of the 1920s

According to Eq. 4.2, an increase in $s(t)$ will, ceteris paribus, decrease $h(t)$, thus reducing the share of labor in each dollar of output and increasing the share of capital. This will, in turn, result in a reduction in overall wage income and an increase in profit or capital income as a share of overall income—that is, an increase in profits per dollar of output. As it turns out, President Herbert Hoover's 1929 *Committee on Recent Economic Changes* examined this very question—that is, the relationship between

Table 6.8 EUD and employment: 1923–1925

	%Change in horsepower per establishment					
	Decrease	*Decrease*	*Increase*	*Increase*	*Increase*	*Increase*
%Change in wage earners per establishment	20–40%	0–20%	0–0%	20–40%	40–60%	60–80%
Decrease						
20–40%	4	12	8	1		
0–20%	8	49	66	15	7	
Increase						
0–20%	5	12	54	25	5	7
20–40%		2	5	10	1	1
40–60%		1	2	1		1

EUD-based investment and employment in the 1920s. Specifically, in a report prepared by Willard Thorp of the *National Bureau of Economic Research*, data for 302 industries from 1923 to 1925 were used to test what at the time was the commonly held view that EUD-based investment was worker-decreasing—that is, the more an industry converted to the new power drive technology, the lower would be the level of employment—precisely the point that Einstein would raise in 1932.

Table 6.8 presents his findings. Of the 302 industries studied, employment decreased in 170, which is astonishing given that GDP growth rates throughout the 1920s varied from 4 to 5.2%.[5] Of these, 97 industries reported an increase in horsepower per establishment (EUD), while 73 reported a decrease. Of the 132 that reported an increase in employment, the majority saw horsepower increase by considerably more than employment. For example, in 25, horsepower increased by 20 to 40%, while employment increased by 0 to 20%.

A number of remarks are in order. First, these results can be misleading given the nature of the new power drive technology. For example, it appears somewhat incongruous that in a period of robust growth, 49 industries would have reported a decrease in both horsepower and employment. In fact, it may have well been the case that the conversion to electric unit drive witnessed a decrease in overall horsepower as smaller motors may have replaced larger ones (driving belts and shafts) whose rated horsepower (potential) had never been fully utilized. As Devine (1983) pointed

[5] Department of Commerce (1975), F31.

out, "Unit drive used less energy than group drive for the same reasons that group drive used less energy than line shaft drive. (Devine, 1983, p. 30)." Another anomaly, according to LaVerne Beales of the Census Bureau was related to the conversion from steam engines to steam turbines, specifically "The lower efficiency of the steam engine and the belt system which usually accompanies it, when compared to the steam turbine used to drive an electric generator, is so considerable that the rated horsepower necessary to do the same work is greater in the first than in the second case." (p. 175). Or, it could be the case that in some of these industries, larger, more-productive EUD-driven firms' market share increased at the expense of smaller firms (and even crowded them out) and that as a result overall horsepower actually decreased, but energy consumption (i.e., *kWhs*) actually increased. Dexter Kimball, in Chap. 2 of the *Report on Recent Economic Changes*, pointed out:

> *An important element in the increase in output has been the rapid abandonment of inefficient plants. In a recent survey of the merchant blast furnace industry, it is reported that of the 37 plants furnishing data for the prewar years 1911-1914, 15 were both hand filled and sand cast, while 34 were both mechanically filled and machine case. But in 1926, out of 49 plants furnishing data, only 3 were both hand filled and sand cast, while 34 were both mechanically filled and machine cast. P. 82*

Acceleration, Rationalization, and Profits
As pointed out earlier, adopting electric unit drive was a profit-increasing strategy regardless of market conditions. Accelerating machine processes reduces unit costs and thus increases profits and profitability. At the aggregate level, the conversion to electric unit drive will, as such, reduce labor's share of income and increase that of capital. As it turned out, this very question was what led to the creation of the NBER and the Brookings Institution. As pointed out earlier, the latter embarked on an ambitious program of estimating the country's potential GDP in the 1930s.

Evidence from the Popular Press

Understandably, acceleration-based increases in productive capacity presented at the time and continue to present a challenge to statisticians and policymakers, owing in large measure to their nonmaterial, invisible, and decidedly abstract nature. While converting to EUD will increase a machine/tool's rated capacity, only when the accelerated machine/tool in question actually is operated at this new, higher capacity will an accurate measure of its overall increase in output (i.e., its potential) be had. That being said, there is every reason to believe that the question of growing excess rated capacity would nonetheless have percolated into the public sphere, via news reports (radio and newspapers).

In this section, anecdotal evidence of the growing presence of excess capacity in the public eye in the 1920s is presented in the form of keyword research. More specifically, keyword searches in two broad categories (excess capacity and wages) were conducted using *The New York Times* from 1901 to 1930.

Excess Capacity

A total of eight keyword (combination of keywords) searches were conducted for six five-year time intervals, notably 1901–1905, 1906–1910, 1911–1915, 1916–1920, 1921–1925, and 1926–1930, using the *ProQuest Search Instrument.* The excess capacity–related keywords and keyword combinations in question were "Excess Capacity," "Over-Production," "Overinvestment," "Mass Production, Unemployment," and "Electricity, Unemployment." The null hypothesis in this case is that the mid-to-late 1920s were no different from the 1900s, 1910s, and early 1920s.

The results presented in Table 6.9 show a sharp increase in the use of the eight keywords and keyword combinations in the 1920s, especially in the period 1926–1930. For example, the use of the keyword "Over-Production" increased from 35 in 1920 to 251 in 1926–1930. Similarly, the use of the keyword "Excess Capacity" went from one in the early 1900s to 36 from 1926 to 1930. While there are obvious limits to this type of analysis, the evidence appears to reject the null hypothesis in favor of the alternative, namely, the presence of excess capacity. Put differently, the evidence from the popular press indicates that the US economy in the late 1920s found itself increasingly in a state of generalized excess capacity. A good example is the following editorial excerpt from the November 9, 1930, edition of *The Washington Post*, entitled "Cause of the Crash."

Table 6.9 The New York Times–based historical keyword survey results, 1900–1930

Keyword	*1901–1905*	*1906–1910*	*1911–1915*	*1916–1920*	*1921–1925*	*1926–1930*
Excess capacity	1	1	3	5	13	36
Overproduction	33	21	32	35	100	251
Overinvestment	2	4	6	5	6	17
Low wage	3	9	24	13	40	76
Fair wage	13	11	22	44	45	40
Mass production, unemployment	0	0	0	0	7	108
Electricity, unemployment	0	0	11	8	32	101

> *Out of many diagnoses of the business depression economist have arrived at the conclusion that the country overproduced in the years immediately preceding the crash more goods than the public could consume with its limited buying power. The resultant surplus became a drug on the market and it was necessary to curtail production while the slack was being taken up.*
>
> *Until now, this has been mere theory. But the figures that have just been worked out by the Census Bureau sustain the theory beyond doubt. The fact that there was overproduction can no longer be questioned. But why did a surplus of goods bring hard times when thousands of people are in need of more clothes, better food, and more substantial houses, as well as the conveniences and luxuries of life?*
>
> *The reason reaches far back into history. In 1849, according to the figures of the Census Bureau, the manufacturing industries of the United States produced goods valued at approximately $1,000,000,000 and $236,755,000 in wages. Since that time both wages and the value of products have increased enormously. In 1929 the output of manufacturing industries reached the highest point in history. Goods turns out by American plants were valued at $68,000,000,000. Had industries paid the same proportion of this return in wages as it did in 1849, wage earners would have received an aggregate of $16,000,000,000. Instead, they were paid $11,271,116,000.*
>
> *In these figures lies the story of the industrial depression. While goods were being turned out at a pace never before equaled in history, the buying power of the public was making small gains.*

The Wage Question

The second keyword search focused on the question of wages, specifically on the extent to which wages were seen as being too low in the public eye, given the perception that productivity was increasing and excess capacity was increasingly becoming a problem. After all, most, like Einstein, understood the notion of balance—or equilibrium—as expressed in Eq. 4.1, namely, that increasing productivity requires a higher income and expenditure in order that balance be maintained. Given the growing perception that the "system" was out of balance, to what extent were wages and wage income seen to be the cause in the popular press? To answer this question, a second keyword search was conducted in *The New York Times* for "Low Wage" and "Fair Wage." The null hypothesis was that references to both keywords would be independent of the chosen time interval. The results are presented in Table 6.5, where the number of references to "Low Wage" increased markedly in the 1920s, while the number of references to "Fair Wage" jumps (doubled) beginning in the late 1910s.

Where Einstein Erred: The Problem Was Not the Distribution of Income, but the Overall Level of Income

By the late 1920s, many observers believed that the inability of the US economy to produce at its newfound capacity owed to the fact that the ratio of profit to overall income had increased—that is, wealth had, in a Thomas Piketty way, become increasingly concentrated in the hands of investors/shareholders, a view shared by Einstein. He went on to argue that this was owed to the power asymmetry between shareholders and workers in favor of the former.

However, as argued in this chapter, this was not the cause but rather the symptom of the failure of overall income to increase commensurately with potential rated capacity, a condition best understood as underincome—that is, the inability of national income to track potential GDP. As shown in the numerical simulation in Chap. 3, an increase in $s(t)$, the index of aggregate, economy-wide operating speed, fails to increase overall income commensurately with the newly found potential, but does increase the ratio of profits to wage income. It is important not to confuse the two, as one is the cause, while the other is the symptom. The key to restoring balance lies in increasing the overall level of income, thus increasing both wage and profit income, and not in increasing wages as a percentage of income.

Summary and Conclusions

This chapter presented evidence of a major capacity-augmenting technology shock in the 1920s. A number of estimation techniques were employed, from simple productivity indices to historical data to theoretical growth model–based estimates. In all cases, the estimates ranged from 20% to 40%, which is admittedly significant. The upshot is straightforward, namely, that the 1920s and 1930s were decades of what can best be described as paradigm technological change, confirming Einstein's basic premise, namely, the presence of "technical progress."

References

Beaudreau, B. C. (1996). *Mass production, the stock market crash, and the great depression: The macroeconomics of electrification*. Greenwood Press.

Chase, S. (1934). *The economy of abundance*. The John Day Company.

Devine, W. D., Jr. (1983). From shafts to wires: Historical perspective on electrification. *The Journal of Economic History, 43*, 347–372.
Douglas, P. H. (1927). The modern technique of mass production and its relation to wages. *Proceedings of the Academy of Political Science in the City of New York, 12*(3), 17–42.
Fisher, I. (1930). *The stock market crash–and after*. The Macmillan Company.
Knight, F. H. (1921). *Risk, uncertainty, and profit*. Houghton Mifflin.
Loeb, H. (1935). *The chart of plenty: A study of America's product capacity based on the findings of the National Survey of potential product capacity*. Viking Press.
Nourse, E. A., et al. (1934). *America's capacity to produce*. Brookings Institution.
Scott, H., et al. (1933). *Introduction to technocracy*. The John Day Company.
Tugwell, R. G. (1927). *Industry's coming of age*. Columbia University Press.
U.S. Department of Commerce. (1975). *Historical statistics of the United States, colonial times to 1970*. U.S. Government Printing Office.

CHAPTER 7

Post-Depression Reckoning

Abstract Not only did Einstein provide an explanation of the causes leading up to and including the Great Depression, but he also provided policy recommendations. This chapter examines their validity in light of the events of the post-Depression period. For example, were his recommendations regarding wages borne out by the events of the post-Depression period?

Keywords Policy recommendations • Wages • Post-Depression developments

Introduction

As mentioned earlier, Einstein's account of the events leading up to and including the Great Depression was summarily dismissed by virtually everyone, then as now. Irving Fisher, with whom he corresponded, dismissed the core of his analysis, all the while agreeing that the 1920s were years of important technical progress. Most observers, then and now, did likewise, some going as far as to argue that while he was a "giant" in the field of theoretical physics, he was a "dwarf" in so far as his understanding of economics was concerned.

While some have pointed to the wisdom of some of his ideas, the general consensus is that he was out of his league. But was he? Was his analysis

B. C. Beaudreau, *Energy, Einstein, and the Great Depression*,
https://doi.org/10.1007/978-3-032-26664-4_7

as "way off" as alleged? Were his predictions totally off? Was he the crank that some allege? This chapter re-examines his diagnosis as well as his prognosis in light of subsequent developments in the post-Depression era, raising the question of whether the conditions that led ultimately to the end of the downturn were consistent with his prognosis. In other words, was the state—that is, conditions—of the post-WWII US economy consistent with his policy recommendations? Or was he completely off base?

Technical Progress

As mentioned, Einstein's theory of the Great Depression was based on the presence of "paradigm" technical progress—that is, major, economy-wide technological change. Unfortunately, he, like many of his contemporaries—economists and business analysts—was unable to identify the exact techniques that were involved. As we have argued in this book, the techniques in question would need to be related to the material processes of wealth and not the basket of goods and services (i.e., product innovation).

That this was the case owed, in large measure, to the fact that mainstream production theory at the time was literally devoid of technique and technology, focusing on labor and capital. More specifically, technique and technology were (and remain so to this day) couched in the production function and thus were seen as parametric—the A scaler in Charles Cobb and Paul Douglas' 1928 production function.

Unfortunately, despite what was an era of radical process innovation, production theory failed to evolve. For the next half century, technique and technology would constitute a black box of sorts, what Moses Abramovitz would refer to as the source of our ignorance. Recently, Harvard University economics professor Gregory Mankiw described it as "primitive," pointing out that "there was a lot we did not understand about production."

This would have made it hard, if not impossible, for Einstein's contemporaries (until his death in 1955) to test his theory. Throughout this period, any evidence was largely anecdotal and involved a lot of arm-waving. However, this changed with the development of modern growth theory, where measures of technique and technological change–based increases in productivity and growth were developed. In short, the latter were measured as the residual in a first-order differentiated Cobb-Douglas aggregate production function. In short, estimates of technique and

Table 7.1 Compound annual average growth rates of output per hour, private domestic and private non-farm economy, United States, 1919–1948

Period	*Private domestic economy*	*Private non-farm economy*
1919–1929	2.36	2.27
1929–1941	2.48	2.35
1941–1948	2.17	1.71

Source: Field (2003, p. 1409)

technological change could be "backed out of" measures of output and input (capital and labor) growth.

In the early 2000s, Alexander Field applied these techniques to historical US time series for the 1920s and 1930s. His results showed that the 1920s and 1930s were decades of record technological change–based productivity and output growth, with the 1930s being the most prosperous decade in so far as productivity growth was concerned. His results are presented in Table 7.1, where we see that productivity growth continued unabated in the 1930s at a rate of 2.48% for the private domestic economy and 2.35% for the private non-farm economy.

Not only do his results corroborate Einstein's (and others) basic premise, it raises the possibility that the technological unemployment that he identified would have been a going concern throughout the 1930s, contributing to exacerbating an already bad situation—that is, increasing technological unemployment. In fact, one could argue that ongoing technical progress would have undone any possible improvement from the myriad policy measures enacted throughout the decade. In other words, any increase in government expenditure would have mixed effects, if not no effect whatsoever, in the presence of ongoing technological change.

This leads us to the conclusion that while the profession is no further today in its ability to identify the exact nature of the process-based technical progress, the basic tenets of growth theory are able to confirm the presence of what could be referred to as significant improvements in material process technology in the 1920s and 1930s.

Labor Productivity and Real Wages

Einstein's main policy prescription was an increase in wages so as to provide the wherewithal to increase consumption—a view hauntingly similar view to that of US industrialist Henry Ford and Boston mass merchandiser Edward A. Filene. While this was not a necessary condition, it could be viewed as a sufficient one. In other words, if wages were to rise commensurately with productivity, then income and expenditure would do likewise. That it is not a necessary condition follows from the fact that overall expenditure could increase in other ways, such as an increase in government spending.

Table 5.2 presents the NBER labor productivity index for manufacturing for the period in question, as well as a measure of the real wage. We see that by 1945, productivity had increased monotonically from the base year of 1923 by 77%. Over the same period, real wages had increased by 68%. From 1923 to 1929, productivity had increased by 25%, while real wages increased by 9%. Nominal wages, on the other hand, had increased by 7%, corroborating Einstein and others' view on the underlying cause of the downturn, namely, the failure of wages to keep pace with productivity growth.

According to this view, full employment could only be achieved if real wages increased commensurately with productivity. The data in Table 7.2 show that the outbreak of war in the late 1930s, with all it entailed, had a salutary effect on the US economy as nominal and real wages increased rapidly in this period. By 1945, productivity in manufacturing had increased by 77% and wages, by 68%. Nominal wages increased by 63% in this period. Clearly, the war did exactly what Einstein had recommended, namely, increase wages and wage income, bringing it in line—more or less—with productivity or what he referred to as technical progress.

Overall Expenditure

As the simulations in Chap. 4 showed, an increase in overall machine and equipment speed ($s(t)$) reduces hours ($h(t)$) and overall output for a given level of autonomous expenditure (i.e., investment expenditure). However, this can be undone by an increase in expenditure, whether by the government or by increasing net exports. For an increase in government spending to be effective, it has to be financed by the sale of debt to the central bank as opposed to taxation or the sale of debt in financial markets, as the latter would simply reduce consumption and investment. Hence, the government would need to either indebt itself vis-à-vis the private banking system or the central bank in order to finance its spending.

Table 7.2 US manufacturing wage and price data, 1923–1945

Year	*Nominal wage*	*CPI*	*Real wage*	*NBER productivity index*
1923	0.52	51.30	1.01	40.2
1924	0.54	51.20	1.05	42.8
1925	0.54	51.90	1.04	45.6
1926	0.54	51.10	1.05	46.5
1927	0.54	50.00	1.08	47.6
1928	0.56	50.80	1.10	49.7
1929	0.56	50.60	1.10	52.0
1930	0.55	49.3	1.11	52.3
1931	0.51	44.8	1.13	54.0
1932	0.44	40.2	1.09	50.5
1933	0.44	39.3	1.11	54.9
1934	0.53	42.2	1.25	57.4
1935	0.54	42.6	1.26	61.2
1936	0.55	42.7	1.28	61.6
1937	0.62	44.5	1.39	60.7
1938	0.62	43.9	1.41	59.9
1939	0.63	43.2	1.45	65.4
1940	0.66	43.9	1.50	68.7
1941	0.73	47.2	1.54	71.2
1942	0.85	53.0	1.60	72.4
1943	0.96	56.8	1.69	73.4
1944	1.01	58.2	1.73	72.5
1945	1.02	59.7	1.70	71.5

Source: US Department of Commerce (1975), Series D802, F5. 1958=100. *Constant 1958 dollars

The outbreak of WWII witnessed a massive increase in autonomous US spending, first by the Allies (via exports of armaments), and then by both the Allies and the US government. So much so that by 1944, US GDP had almost doubled vis-à-vis 1929. An astonishing outcome by any account—in fact, historic—and further evidence of Einstein's view that the US's ability to create wealth had increased substantially, but that income and expenditure levels were such that it could not produce at its potential.

Assuming that these constraints had been lifted—or at least, pushed back—by 1944, simple growth theory would peg the overall effect of Einstein's technical progress at between 35% and 45%, more than double the estimates obtained by the Brookings Institution and the Loeb report in the early 1930s.

Summary and Conclusions

This chapter examined Einstein's prescriptions for an end to the Great Depression in light of economic conditions at the end of World War II, the idea being to evaluate whether or not they were consistent with the conditions of full employment (i.e., in the post-WWII years). The focus was on wages, as higher wages were the main element of his overall policy prescriptions. It was shown that throughout the 1920s, nominal and real wages in manufacturing lagged behind productivity, but that by the end of WWII, they had caught up, pointing to the fact that the war effort had done what the private, for-profit economy had not been able to do in the 1920s and 1930s.

That this was the case provides an excellent segue into the next chapter, which examines Einstein's writings on the broader question of capitalism versus socialism, writings that continued after WWII. Like the members of President Roosevelt's Brains Trust in 1933, he struggled with the various trade-offs between the benefits of free enterprise (e.g., innovation, initiative, and freedom) and the benefits of coordinated, top-down government intervention.

References

Field, A. J. (2003). The most technologically progressive decade of the century. *American Economic Review, 93*(4), 1399–1413.

U.S. Department of Commerce. (1975). *Historical statistics of the United States, colonial times to 1970.* U.S. Government Printing Office.

CHAPTER 8

Einstein on Capitalism Versus Socialism

Abstract Albert Einstein's interest in the Great Depression led to a life-long interest in the merits of capitalism versus socialism. Chief among his concerns was the ability of a free-market economy to navigate the transition to higher growth and income in the face of technical progress. Pointing to a command economy's superior ability to translate potential into actual GDP, he would go on to weigh this against the associated loss of freedom (scientific, technological).

Keywords Capitalism • Socialism • Coordination • Innovation • Freedom

Introduction

While Einstein's interest in the Great Depression appears to have waned in the mid-1930s, he nonetheless kept an iron in the proverbial economics fire in the subsequent years, writing extensively on the capitalism-socialism debate. In this chapter, it is argued that his interest in this debate stemmed ultimately from his view/diagnosis of the causes of the Great Depression, specifically, his interest in the ability of capitalism to deliver the benefits of new, more productive production technologies.

B. C. Beaudreau, *Energy, Einstein, and the Great Depression*, https://doi.org/10.1007/978-3-032-26664-4_8

While there is no hard evidence of this other than the fact that he was a trained physicist, it could be argued that the problem was in many regards one of Lagrangian mechanics where the Lagrangian L is defined as the difference between the kinetic energy T and the potential energy V of a system: $L = T - V$. The potential energy V is a function of the system's generalized coordinates (and possibly time), representing the potential for doing work within the system. In his mind, T corresponds to actual US GDP, while V corresponds to potential US GDP (see Chap. 6). The debate is, in essence, over the Lagrangian multiplier, namely, the role of institutions in translating potential US GDP into actual US GDP, of maximizing T and minimizing V.

The analysis will be based, in large measure, on his 1949 *Monthly Review* article entitled "Why Socialism?" The chosen framework will be a simple Nash wage game in the presence of electric unit drive–based productivity and output growth, allowing us to identify analytically the main elements of his argument.

The upshot is that he had anticipated a number of the debates that raged throughout the 1930s without knowing it. For example, his analysis is not unlike that of New Deal Brains Truster Rexford G. Tugwell, who in the Industrial Discipline and the Governmental Arts, published in 1933, addressed the question of the profit motive and the need, in time of paradigm technological change, for government. In other regards, it is similar in scope to the technocracy movement in the early 1930s that called for a similar reorganization of industry and society.

Productivity, Wages, and Incentives

The gist of Einstein's interest in socialism can be understood in terms of the following Nash wage game. Simply put, a Nash game is one in which players choose their strategies independently of each other. In this case, companies choose both the wage they pay their workers $w_i(t)$ as well as the number of hours $h_i(t)$. To simplify the analysis, it is assumed that there are n companies in our hypothetical economy and that each company's revenue is $1/n^{\text{th}}$ of total income, defined as $\sum_{i=1}^{n} w_i(t)h_i(t)$. The ith company's profits are given as $\pi_i(t) = 1/n\sum_{i=1}^{n} w_i(t)h_i(t) - w_i(t)h_i(t)$.

Now, suppose that all n firms adopt electric unit drive which increases machine speed by 30%. As pointed out in Chap. 5, this implies that the *i*th company can now serve the market with 30% fewer h, raising the question: What should the representative company do, and what will it do? From a social welfare point of view, given that output per h has now increased by 30%, it could raise the wage by an equivalent amount. This would lead to a 30% increase in aggregate income and a 30% increase in the company's market demand. This will be referred to as the cooperative outcome.

However, in a Nash setting, there are no incentives to do so for the simple reason that by raising the wage by 30%, ceteris paribus, costs will rise by an equivalent amount, but market share will not. In fact, revenue will only increase by $1/n^{\text{th}}$ of the increase. Put differently, there are no private incentives to increase wages and income. This will be referred to as the Nash or market equilibrium.

Given that output per worker hour has increased by 30%, there is every reason to believe that the ith company will cut hours by 30%, reducing costs by an equivalent percentage, but only reducing revenue by a fraction (i.e., $1/n$). This will be referred to as technological unemployment.

The last point has to do with the legitimacy of productivity-based wage increases. In this game, as was the case throughout the 1920s and 1930s, wages should follow productivity. However, as was shown in Chap. 3, labor in most of the nineteenth century and in virtually all of the twentieth century was an organizational input, overseeing the workings of complex and increasingly productive (owing to acceleration) machinery and equipment. By 1890, British economist Alfred Marshall, as well as the London Board of Trade, referred to workers as machine operatives. In short, workers no longer powered the machinery and equipment of the twentieth century.

This creates a fundamental indeterminacy as wages in for-profit market economies are the medium by which wealth is monetized and incomized. That is, demand for goods and services originates in the payments companies make to their machine supervisors. However, as technical progress is, in most instances, unrelated to what could be referred to as labor tasks, this creates a fundamental indeterminacy. As profit income is a residual, there is virtually no way to increase income and expenditure in response to a massive shock like electric unit drive–based material process acceleration.

Income Indeterminacy in its Historical Context

This indeterminacy is not new but rather has a history that dates back to the beginnings of industrialization. In short, how to incomize wealth when labor is no longer physically productive and has been reduced to a supervisory input? As far back as 1819, Swiss political economist Jean-Charles-Léonard Simonde de Sismondi had pointed this out. In his words

> *Le vendeur n'a pas par lui-même aucun moyen d'étendre son débit, qui ne réagisse sur ses confrères; il leur dispute une quantité donnée de revenu qui doit remplacer son capital; et plus, il réussit à en garder pour lui-même; moins il en laisse pour les autres. Il ne dépend nullement du producteur d'augmenter les revenus de la société, ou du marché qu'il sert de manière qu'ils puissent s'échanger contre une augmentation de produits .... Entre commerçants, on regarde comme une mauvaise action de se séduire réciproquement ses pratiques; mais la concurrence que chacun exerce contre tous ne présente point une idée aussi précise; et un commerçant n'a pas moins d'empressement d'étendre son débit aux dépens de ses confrères qu'à le proportionner à l'accroissement des richesses, lorsque celles-ci lui offrent à l'échange d'un nouveau revenu. Jusqu'ici dans l'un ou l'autre cas, la découverte d'un procédé nouveau a causé une grande perte nationale, une grande diminution de revenu, et par conséquent, la consommation. (Simonde,* 1819, *p. 318)*[1]

US automobile magnate Henry Ford, founder of the Ford Motor Company and father of the Model-T, found himself in the midst of a productivity revolution which he attributed to speed (see reference in Chap. 2). Despite the lack of any training in game theory, he was well aware of the problem, namely, one of raising wages in line with overall productivity. From very early on, he realized that for the speed-based Industrial Revolution to be successful, wages and overall income would need to rise.

[1] The seller has no means of expanding his sales by himself, except by affecting his competitors; he is disputing a given amount of income that must replace his capital; and moreover, he succeeds in keeping some for himself; the less he leaves for others. It does not depend at all on the producer to increase society's income, or on the market he serves, in such a way that they can be exchanged for an increase in products.... Among merchants, it is considered bad practice to try to lure each other's clientele; but the competition that each exerts against all does not present such a precise idea; and a merchant is no less eager to expand his sales at the expense of his colleagues than to align them with the increase of wealth, when the latter offers him the exchange of a new income. Up to this point, in either case, the discovery of a new method has caused a great national loss, a large decrease in income, and consequently, consumption (Simonde de Sismondi 1819, p. 318).

As if to show the way, in January 1914, he unilaterally doubled the wages of his Highland Park plant workers and invited his fellow industrialists to do likewise. Not surprisingly, few did. Undeterred, he continued throughout the next decades to plead for higher wages. For example, when invited to the White House by President Herbert Hoover to discuss the depression, he responded as follows:

> *We need to increase the purchasing power of our principal customers, the American people. This can be done in two ways: first, by putting additional value into goods or reducing prices to the level of actual values; and second, a movement to increase the general wage level. Nearly everything in this country is too high priced. The only thing that should be high priced in this country is the man who works. Wages must not come done, they must not even stay at their present level, they must go up. (Fisher,* 1930, *p. 25)*

In many ways, Ford's experience was at the heart of Einstein's interest in the debate over institutions. While Ford continued to believe that the coordination game described above could be solved by his fellow businessmen, it was clear that it could not and would not in a private, for-profit Nash setting. However, like Einstein, Ford was not especially bullish on a government-imposed, across-the-board wage increase, as evidenced by his vehement opposition to President Roosevelt's National Industrial Recovery Act. In his words

> *We've got to stop the gouging process if we want to see all the people reasonably prosperous. There is only one rule of industrialists and that is: Make the best quality goods possible at the lowest cost paying the highest wage possible. Nothing can be right in this country until wages are right. The life of business comes forth from the people in orders. The factories are not stopped for lack of money but for lack of orders. Money loaned at the top means nothing. Money spent at the bottom starts everything. I think that if the industrial leaders had been willing to push wages up during the last thirty years, the present ills would at least not be as great as they are. If the government can help in these matters, well and good, but the government has not a rosy record in running itself so far. New York Times, June 16, 1933*

Just how companies in general would respond to a massive technology shock was on the minds of not only leading industrialists like Ford, but of academics and governments. One such academic was renowned University of Chicago economics professor Thorstein Veblen. Unlike many of his colleagues, he had a keen interest in technology, specifically in technological change. Foremost in his mind, however, was how productivity growth would translate into higher GDP and higher income.

On this very subject, he was categorical. The for-profit economy was fundamentally flawed. In short, there were no reasons to raise output, income, and expenditure. As shown above, companies had no incentives to raise wages. Rather, they were wont to decrease employment as Einstein would point out later in the depths of the downturn. He referred to behavior as a form of "sabotage" in the sense that companies, by cutting employment in response to greater productivity, effectively sabotaged the transition.

That is, instead of raising overall purchasing power commensurately with the newfound ability to produce, they have a tendency to reduce employment, which, as Einstein pointed out, reduces overall income, setting in motion a downward spiral (see Table 4.2).[2]

> *It is a matter of course and of absolute necessity to the conduct of business, that any discretionary businessman must be free to deal or not to deal in any given case; to limit or withhold the equipment under his control, without reservation. Business discretion and business strategy, in fact, has no other means by to work out its aims. So that, in effect, all business sagacity reduces itself in the last analysis to judicious use of sabotage. (Veblen, 1921)*

In light of this, he went on to argue that for-profit market economies were plagued by coordination problems—failures—and as such should be replaced by a new governing class of managers schooled in engineering techniques whose principal goal would be to maximize overall wealth, not profits.[3] These ideas would inspire a group of Columbia University engineering professors to launch, a decade late, the technocracy movement.

The Underpinnings of the National Industrial Recovery Act of 1933 (First New Deal)

Clamoring about the ability of a for-profit economy to make the transition to the new, higher level of wealth had, for most of the 1920s, died down

[2] Jean-Charles-Léonard Simonde de Sismondi (1819) made a similar point, arguing, "Jusqu'ici, dans l'un et l'autre cas, la découverte d'un procédé nouveau a causé une grande perte nationale, une grande diminution de revenu, et, par conséquent, de consommation." (Simonde de Sismondi 1819, p. 321).

[3] In short, their problem would be to maximize output/wealth, not profits.

owing to the robust growth of the decade, a decade known as the Roaring Twenties. While Europe found itself in shambles, North America was enjoying unprecedented growth. However, the late twenties showed troubling signs as labor markets began to weaken. Sensing growing weakness, the Republican Party under Senator Reed Smoot turned to an upward tariff revision to create "space" in the US market for capacity-laden companies. To his way of thinking, productivity—what he referred to as efficiency—had increased well beyond demand. Restricting foreign access to the US market would create the necessary room to fully employ all labor and capital. In short, the Republican response to excess capacity was to restrict access to the home market.

The Stock Market Crash of October 1929 and the ensuing descent into what would become the worst downturn of all time galvanized the nation in the early 1930s. The debate over the ability of a for-profit economy to make the transition to the new, higher level of GDP gave way to one over the stock market crash and the ensuing freefall of investment expenditure. Many pointed to the prophecies of radical thinkers like Karl Marx—the for-profit economy was fundamentally unstable. Few made the connection between excess capacity and the vertiginous decrease in investment in the 1930s.

One of those few was Columbia University economics professor Rexford G. Tugwell who held that the key to understanding the downturn was the technology shock of the 1920s. The inability to make the transition, he argued, translated into a decrease in employment and investment. After all, why invest in new greenfield capacity when existing capacity is underutilized? The depression, he argued, had its origins in the disequilibrium of the 1920s—in short, it was the culmination of the many divergent forces at work, namely, growing potential and shrinking demand.

Long story short, Tugwell's writings caught the eye of New York Senator Robert F. Wagner and New York Governor Franklin D. Roosevelt. Chosen as the Party's presidential candidate, Roosevelt ran on a platform that was largely inspired by Tugwell, a program that called for all-around higher wages and short-term government assistance in the form of employment-creating programs. Such were the key elements of what would become the New Deal. In its first incarnation—the National Industrial Recovery Act of 1933—it would call for industry cooperation (i.e., Codes of Fair Competition), higher wages, price fixing, pro-union legislation, and roughly $2 billion in government programs.

Einstein's "why Socialism"

Albert Einstein's "Why Socialism" can be seen as the fruit of a decade-old reflection on this conundrum. In essence, the article consists of an attempt on his part to attribute the Nash outcome described above to a "deficiency" in social behavior, one whose origins and development are remarkably similar to those of Karl Marx—that is, rooted in class conflict. In fact, most of the underlying analysis is based on the labor theory of value.

The article is structured as follows. To begin with, he presents a number of reasons "to express views on the subject of socialism." To begin, he points to the problem as being one of moral philosophy—that is, having to do with the fundamental nature of *Homo sapiens.* Drawing from Thorstein Veblen, he refers to something called the "predatory phase" of human development. He then goes on to describe man as both solitary and social, setting the stage for his main argument of the breakdown of the social element. This is compounded by the fact that change is arduous and difficult.

As a result, the primal egotistical side of man has come to dominate the cooperative side, resulting in a breakdown.

> *I have now reached the point where I may indicate briefly what to me constitutes the essence of the crisis of our time. It concerns the relationship of the individual to society. The individual has become more conscious than ever of his dependence upon society. But he does not experience this dependence as a positive asset, as an organic tie, as a protective force, but rather as a threat to his natural rights, or even to his economic existence. Moreover, his position in society is such that the egotistical drives of his make-up are constantly being accentuated, while his social drives, which are by nature weaker, progressively deteriorate. All human beings, whatever their position in society, are suffering from this process of deterioration. Unknowingly prisoners of their own egotism, they feel insecure, lonely, and deprived of the naive, simple, and unsophisticated enjoyment of life. Man can find meaning in life, short and perilous as it is, only through devoting himself to society.*
>
> *The economic anarchy of capitalist society as it exists today is, in my opinion, the real source of the evil. We see before us a huge community of producers the members of which are unceasingly striving to deprive each other of the fruits of their collective labor—not by force, but on the whole in faithful compliance with legally established rules. In this respect, it is important to realize that the means of production—that is to say, the entire productive capacity that is needed for producing consumer goods as well as additional capital goods—may legally be, and for the most part are, the private property of individuals. (Einstein, 1949 , p. 4)*

The economic anarchy of capitalist society manifests itself in the labor market. Drawing from the labor theory of value, he points to the presence of a widening gap between the value that workers produce and their remuneration. This, he argues, owes to the growing concentration of capital, creating a power imbalance between workers and shareholders.

> *Private capital tends to become concentrated in few hands, partly because of competition among the capitalists, and partly because technological development and the increasing division of labor encourage the formation of larger units of production at the expense of smaller ones. The result of these developments is an oligarchy of private capital the enormous power of which cannot be effectively checked even by a democratically organized political society. This is true since the members of legislative bodies are selected by political parties, largely financed or otherwise influenced by private capitalists who, for all practical purposes, separate the electorate from the legislature. The consequence is that the representatives of the people do not in fact sufficiently protect the interests of the underprivileged sections of the population. Moreover, under existing conditions, private capitalists inevitably control, directly or indirectly, the main sources of information (press, radio, education). It is thus extremely difficult, and indeed in most cases quite impossible, for the individual citizen to come to objective conclusions and to make intelligent use of his political rights. (Einstein, 1949, p. 5)*

Having dismissed the political system as ineffective in dealing with the growing concentration of power, he then turns to the proposed solution, a planned socialist economy.

> *Production is carried on for profit, not for use. There is no provision that all those able and willing to work will always be in a position to find employment; an "army of unemployed" almost always exists. The worker is constantly in fear of losing his job. Since unemployed and poorly paid workers do not provide a profitable market, the production of consumers' goods is restricted, and great hardship is the consequence. Technological progress frequently results in more unemployment rather than in an easing of the burden of work for all. The profit motive, in conjunction with competition among capitalists, is responsible for an instability in the accumulation and utilization of capital which leads to increasingly severe depressions. Unlimited competition leads to a huge waste of labor, and to that crippling of the social consciousness of individuals which I mentioned before. (Einstein, 1949, p. 6)*

Socialism, Freedom, and Innovation

Absent from what has to be considered to be his defining work on socialism is the question of freedom and innovation, a topic he broached in his earlier reflections on free market economies versus command, top-down ones.

> *Logically the simplest but also the riskiest method for attaining this condition is a complete fixed plan or method: the production and distribution of the necessities of life by means of the community. This is materially what to-day is being tried in Russia, and much in the future will depend upon what results will mature from this tremendous experiment.*
> *To expound prophecies along this line would, however, be presumptuous.*
> *Does such a system, for instance, permit production equally as efficient as that which allows the initiative of the individual more liberty?*
> *Again, can this system be maintained at al without the reign of terror that has been maintained up to this time and to which not one of us, oriented "westwardly" would wish to expose himself?*
> *Doesn't such a rigid centralized economic system, too, lean towards protectionism and isolation as against advantageous innovations?*
> *One must consider these things but one must care not to allow such doubts to become prejudices which might prevent the formation of objective judgement.*
> *I personally believe that the whole of these methods are to be preferred which respect traditions and customs to the utmost possible degree compatible with the aim in view. I also believe that any rapid change to public ownership is disadvantageous in the interest of the production of goods; private initiative should be allowed its field of activity, except in so far as it hasn't already been cast aside by economy as the result of cartelization.*
> *In all cases restriction of free unhampered economy is necessary in two respects: the working week in all individual branches must be shortened law, so unemployment will be abolished systematically, and in fixing minimum wages, care must be taken that the buying power of workers corresponds to production.*
> *Furthermore, the price-fixing of these branches of production which have attained a monopolistic character through the organization of the producers should be controlled by the state to the extent of keeping capital accumulation withing a reasonable limit and preventing any artificial restriction of production and consumption.*
> *In this way, it would probably be possible to establish an equilibrium between production and consumption without too great a restriction of free initiative and at the same time eliminate the disproportionate superiority of the owners of the means of production machinery over wage earners (in the widest sense).*

What is patently obvious is the equivocal nature of his thoughts on the question of a free market versus a command economy. On the one hand, he points to the fact that a "rigid centralized economic system" leans toward "protectionism and isolation" and "against advantageous innovations." In the closing paragraph, he describes what can be considered a "best-of-both-worlds" scenario, namely, "establishing an equilibrium between production and consumption without too great a restriction of free initiative." That is solving the coordination failure described above without compromising "free initiative." In other words, control where and when needed, but freedom and initiative otherwise.[4]

Just why he chose not to broach the question can be attributed to a number of factors, not the least of which is the journal and the event, namely, the 1949 inaugural number of a new journal dedicated to socialism and communism, namely, the *Monthly Review* (Einstein, 1949). Clearly, judging from his earlier musings, he felt that command economies were not overly conducive to invention and innovation, owing to the lack of incentives and possibilities.

Analysis

Perhaps the best way to understand "Why Socialism" is as an amalgam of Karl Marx's *Das Kapital* and his earlier writings on technological unemployment. Whereas in the early 1930s he pointed to the unemployment that resulted from "technical progress," here he is attributing it to a breakdown in social values and the emergence of oligarchy, not to mention the overemphasis in education on competition.

His understanding of post-WWI material processes does not appear to have evolved from his early 1930 writings. The labor theory of value remains the cornerstone. Like Marx, he alleges a form of theft on the part of companies as they appropriate the lion's share of workers' productivity.

What is surprising is the extent to which the gist of his argument, namely, that wages had not increased commensurately with productivity, is refuted by wage developments in the 1940s, where the average wage in

[4] One could argue that this view is somewhat autobiographical in the sense that his contributions in physics were, in large measure, the result of academic freedom without which the theory of relativity may have never seen the day. Yet he realized that the only way to enforce the cooperative equilibrium was through control.

manufacturing in the USA doubled, ushering in the greatest period of prosperity in the history of the Western world, namely, the Golden Age of Capitalism. This seems to indicate that he had not kept abreast of the more recent developments but had chosen to explore in more detail the purported conspiratorial side of capitalism.

It could be argued that the problem that he had identified was real (i.e., the coordination failure described above), but that his analysis was not only disturbingly simple but also disconnected from the reality of the 1920s and 1930s. In other words, not only did he, as a physicist, fail to understand the nature of wealth-producing material processes, but he appeared to be somewhat oblivious to the period literature of his day. All of the concepts discussed (and more) in "Why Socialism" had been broached by myriad writers in the intervening two decades.

But, in his defense, it could be argued that this was the way he worked—independently, letting his imagination get the better of him over facts.

Summary and Conclusion

This chapter has examined in detail Albert Einstein's foray into the debate over capitalism and socialism, focusing on an article published twenty years after the start of the Great Depression.

What is interesting is the fact that the bulk of his case for socialism was not the question of equality or exploitation, but rather the coordination failure described in this chapter. Another way to see this is that if businessmen had heeded Henry Ford's call to raise wages commensurately with productivity, there would be no case to be made for socialism, at least according to Albert Einstein. By 1949, wages had doubled relative to their 1929 level.

What is astonishing is the extent to which Einstein had anticipated each of these measures. In fact, it could be argued that his analysis was more complete as it pointed to a form of underincome as opposed to the underconsumption found in the NIRA. Like Einstein who deliberated over the limits of free enterprise—and its costs in terms of innovation—in a top-down command economy, the architects of the NIRA (i.e., the Brains Trust) attempted to lessen the consequences (i.e., government intervention) by inviting companies to set up committees (within their respective industries) to come up with what were known as Codes of Fair Competition, agreements that would govern wages, prices, hours, and investment in the industry in question.

References

Einstein, A. (1949). Why socialism? *Monthly Review, 1*(1), 9–15. https://ssrn.com/abstract=456824236

Fisher, I. (1930). *The stock market crash–and after*. The Macmillan Company.

Simonde de Sismondi, J. C. L. (1819). *Nouveaux Principes d'Économie Politique*. Delaunay.

Veblen, T. (1921). *The engineers and the price system*. Huebsch.

CHAPTER 9

The Structural Impediments to Incomizing Potential Output

Abstract Without being aware of it, Einstein's forays into the causes of the Great Depression were just one of a long series of writings on the problem of incomizing potential output, one that dates back to the early nineteenth century. This chapter examines the various structural impediments to successful transitions to new, higher equilibrium growth paths in response to power drive–based innovations. It is shown that the problem is more complex than previously believed.

Keywords Transitions • Impediments • Incomizing potential output

Introduction

To Einstein and other writers in the 1920s and 1930s, the problem was rather straightforward, namely, one of increasing wages commensurately with productivity. Specifically, they argued that the owners of capital—the shareholders—had appropriated the bulk of these gains, resulting in greater and greater profits.

B. C. Beaudreau, *Energy, Einstein, and the Great Depression*, https://doi.org/10.1007/978-3-032-26664-4_9

However, this view, commonly found in the underconsumption literature, is intrinsically flawed for a number of reasons.[1] First and foremost, it assumes that both labor and capital are physically productive—a by-product of flawed nineteenth-century production theory. As pointed out in Chap. 3, such a view stands in violation of the basic laws of physics, the most salient of which is that energy and energy alone is the only physically productive input. Capital is the equivalent of tools, while labor is, in an industrial setting, the equivalent of what Alfred Marshall referred to as "machine operatives" or machine operators.[2]

This leads to a conundrum; as in the case that concerns us, the conversion to electric unit drive and the resulting increase in operating speeds and productivity have nothing to do with either the tools or operators—rather, it has everything to do with the rents or payoff from greater and greater energy use. When companies chose to convert to electric unit drive, they saw no logical reason to increase wages—workers were simply doing what they had been doing.

Second, because profits are a residual factor payment, paid after markets have cleared (i.e., companies have sold their product), it stands to reason that because wages don't follow productivity, overall income cannot increase. In other words, because shareholders are not paid a "wage" prior to markets clearing, there is no conceivable way to increase overall income. However, once companies begin cutting hours and employment, profits as a share of existing levels of income will increase.

In this chapter, the focus is on structural impediments to incomizing potential output in for-profit economies.[3] As argued, the problem is as old as political economy itself, having a history dating back to Adam Smith. Hence, what Einstein was describing was just another of a long list of what could be referred to as failed transitions to acceleration-induced increases

[1] There were exceptions, the most celebrated of which was Henry Ford who advocated increasing wages for what were macroeconomic reasons. His reasoning was simple: For electric unit drive–based mass production to be successful, expenditure would need to increase in step with output, and for that to occur, wages would need to rise—leading, of course, to the five-dollar day. Ultimately, what he was arguing is that the productivity gains that resulted from acceleration and greater speeds should be shared with workers despite the fact that they were in no way responsible for the gains in question.

[2] In pre-industrial times, workers actually worked in the sense that they expended human energy (i.e., brawn) in transforming raw materials into useful goods.

[3] The term incomizing refers to the ability to increase overall income in lock-step with potential output. For example, if acceleration increases output by 30 percent, then income would have to increase by 30 percent. For more on this, see Beaudreau (2007).

in potential output—or the ability to produce wealth. To begin, the chapter presents the productivity-based remuneration indeterminacy which describes the basic structural impediment to incomizing potential output and, thus, what shall be referred to as the most fundamental flaw in for-product economies.

The Productivity-Based Remuneration Indeterminacy

The indeterminacy, simply put, maintains that in a pure productivity-based income distribution rule, acceleration and greater operating speeds cannot be realized for the lack of income and expenditure. As there are no reasons to increase wages and payments to the owners of capital are a residual (Knight, 1921), income finds itself in a state of inertia.

This constitutes a fundamental flaw in the organization of market economies, namely, the inability to monetize potential output in times of acceleration-based productivity growth. This was the case in the early nineteenth century when many a writer pointed to the failure of wages to increase in response to the introduction of steam engine–based acceleration. This can manifest itself in two ways. First, the inability to monetize potential output could act as a constraint, leading forward-looking companies to forego adopting the new technology outright. Or it could lead companies that have adopted it to cut hours and employment. The former leads to status-quo inertia, where the level of income remains constant, while the latter leads to an Einsteinian downturn as companies cut hours and employment and the economy enters a downward spiral (see Table 4.2).

Underincome and the Inevitable Downturn

This failure, as was shown in Chap. 5, leads inevitably to a downturn as companies reduce operating hours and employment in the hope of increasing profits. After all, now if operating speeds increase by 20%, they can supply their market with 20% fewer operating hours. As mentioned, Thorstein Veblen referred to this as a form of sabotage, when, in actual fact, it was simply the result of the profit motive and common sense. Why continue operating at 100% when 20% of your output will not be sold?

Karl Marx referred to the same behavior as evidence of class conflict—capitalists introduced new techniques (i.e., the steam engine) with the explicit intention of increasing the rate of surplus value. To the untrained eye, this will appear to be the case. However, it should be seen as a consequence of the very way in which capitalism evolved in the presence of acceleration-based productivity gains.

Solving the Indeterminacy: History and Theory

The problem, simply put, consists of increasing income commensurately with potential output in a world in which neither labor nor capital is theoretically (i.e., physically) responsible for the increase and in which there are no private incentives to increase wages.

Table 9.1 presents a non-exhaustive listing of authors who addressed the problem and the proposed solutions. Atop the list is Adam Smith who referred to the indeterminacy as "specialization is determined by the extent of the market," by which it should be understood that the presence of a new drive technology (i.e., the steam engine) is not a sufficiency condition for income and output to increase, but that the decision to convert to the new technology is limited by the "extent of the market." The solution, he argued, was free trade as a way in which to increase the "extent" of the market—in short, extending the market.

British industrialist Robert Owen waded into the debate, arguing that weakness in the economy in the 1810s owed to scientific progress, by which it should be understood the steam engine. To him, wages failed to

Table 9.1 Proposed solutions to the indeterminacy: the historical record

Author	*Diagnosis*	*Solution*
Adam smith	Specialization is determined by the extent of the market	Extend the market via free trade
Robert Owen	Scientific power has increased productivity without a commensurate increase in income	Replace money with labor certificates in an amount equal to overall output and distribute to workers
Henry ford	Wages are too low	Raise wages without third-party coercion
Paul Douglas	Output exceeds income	Estimate scientific labor and capital output elasticities. Use as a basis to argue in favor of higher wages
Technocrats	Innovations in energy use have increased capacity beyond the ability to take the goods off the market	Replace money with energy certificates in the amount of available energy. Distribute equally among the population

keep pace with productivity and output. In light of this flaw, he proposed a radical program of replacing money and money prices with labor certificates that would be issued and distributed by a third party in the amount of potential output—in other words, resolving the indeterminacy. University of Chicago professor Paul Douglas also raised the indeterminacy in the 1920s and set out to resolve it by invoking what he referred to as the laws of production by which it should be understood that labor and capital's output elasticities stood at 0.75% and 0.25%, respectively, providing a scientific basis for wage setting.[4] Specifically, labor was responsible for—and hence entitled to—75% of national income, while capital's share was 25%. Hence, the overall wage bill should correspond to 75% of productivity gains, with capital at 25%.

The US technocrats, a collection of socially minded engineers, were very damning in their criticism, arguing that the economics profession had failed on all accounts to understand the "nature and causes of the wealth of nations" and the indeterminacy referred to in this chapter. Looking at things from an engineering (i.e., applied physics) point of view, they argued that neoclassical production theory was fundamentally flawed as it violated basic physics. Energy, they argued, was the key input. As for the indeterminacy, they proposed, much like Owen, a complete overhaul of the monetary system, replacing money with energy certificates and prices with relative energy prices. Income would be distributed by the technate in an egalitarian fashion. As the quantity of energy certificates would be tied to energy availability (and use), the indeterminacy described here would be nonexistent.

Table 9.2 presents a listing of the various ways in which the indeterminacy can or could be resolved and each's sustainability. The first is the issuance and distribution of bank-created consumer credit. Unfortunately, this solution is not sustainable as it amounts, over time, to a transfer of wealth from workers to shareholders. Ultimately, workers' after-credit-payment income would go to zero, and shareholders' percentage of overall income would go to 100. The second is bank-financed government expenditure. As pointed out, this would only be successful if the government is able to tax back the entire amount and repeat the operation year after year.

[4] The Cobb-Douglas production function and estimates were motivated not by a desire to further understand production, but by what he saw as the failure of income to increase in step with potential output in the 1920s.

Table 9.2 Theoretically possible solutions

Solution	*Description*	*Sustainable or not*
Raise wages by fiat	Sharing of energy rents	Sustainable
Introduce sales credit	Roundabout way to increase income. The population is increasingly indebted	Not sustainable
Bank-financed government expenditure	Government would indebt itself by the amount of the increase and use the proceeds to firm up product markets	Only sustainable if the government is able to tax back the entire amount and use it in subsequent years. Otherwise, inflationary
Price energy at its marginal revenue product	Companies would use bank credit to purchase the increase in output. The resulting revenue would then be redistributed to the owners of labor and capital	Sustainable
Price deflation proportional to the increased productivity	Assumes that companies will produce at capacity, flood the market with the additional output, and then cut prices to clear the market	Sustainable, but unlikely

The third solution consists of pricing energy at its marginal product and distributing the rents to the owners of labor and capital—a solution similar in scope to the technocrats. The last solution is generalized proportionate price deflation. That is, a 20% increase in acceleration-based potential output would be combined with a 20% decrease in prices, holding nominal wages constant.

Problem Remains Unresolved

Unfortunately, the problem of incomizing potential output in times of paradigm technological change remains both obscure and unresolved to this day. Today, as in the past, most believe that an increase in potential output automatically increases income by an equivalent amount—unlike Adam Smith, Robert Owen, Jean-Charles-Léonard Simonde de Sismondi, and others.

As shown, to understand the problem requires a knowledge of the physics of wealth-generating material processes as well as an understanding of the monetization of output and its role in overall expenditure. Unfortunately, Albert Einstein fell short on both fronts, despite being one of the greatest minds of all time.

Summary and Conclusions

Little did Albert Einstein know, but the problem he had stumbled upon was one whose history extended back in time to the beginning of the industrial age. That he was unable to identify its very cause, nor provide a genuine solution, should come as no surprise. Rather, his writings should be seen as an independently arrived-at rehash of the writing of many a nineteenth- and twentieth-century political economist. Had he had knowledge of this literature, perhaps he could have made a genuine, enlightened contribution, being the trained mind he was. But instead, he chose, in his later years, to focus on class conflict.

References

Beaudreau, B. C. (2007). *Underincome: When markets fail to monetize output.* iUnivderse.

Knight, F. (1921). *Risk, uncertainty and profit.* Houghton Mifflin Co., The Riverside Press.

CHAPTER 10

Summary and Conclusions

Abstract This chapter summarizes and concludes the analysis. This book has provided a reexamination of physicist Albert Einstein's forays into the causes and consequences of the Great Depression. In short, his understanding of both the causes and consequences is analyzed in terms of a kinetics-augmented macroeconomic model of the U.S. economy in the late 1920s and early 1930s. The technical progress that he invoked was identified as the introduction of a new power-drive technology in the form of electric unit drive. A discussion of his life-long interest in institutions (i.e. free markets versus socialism) is also provided.

Keywords Albert Einstein • Great Depression • Technical progress • Conclusions

In their 2004 article entitled "The Stock Market Boom Was Not a Bubble: Irving Fisher Was Right" published in the *International Economic Review*, 2004 Nobel Prize laureate Edward Prescott and Ellen McGrattan argued that Yale University economics professor Irving Fisher was right to point out that the stock market boom of the late 1920s was not a bubble, but rather was the result of vastly improved fundamentals. This book has done likewise with celebrated physicist and

B. C. Beaudreau, *Energy, Einstein, and the Great Depression*,
https://doi.org/10.1007/978-3-032-26664-4_10

1921 Nobel laureate Albert Einstein's forays into the debate over the causes of the Great Depression, arguing that he was right to point to "technical progress" as the cause but that like Irving Fisher's view of the causes of the 1928–1929 stock market boom, he was unable to identify the exact technological advance(s) at play and how it/they would contribute to the worse downturn in history.

Like Einstein, Fisher took an active interest in the Great Depression. While he agreed with Einstein that the 1920s had been a decade of great technological change (not specified), he disagreed over the actual cause of the downturn. Rather, he put the blame on price deflation in the presence of sizable levels of nominal debt (i.e., the debt-deflation theory), while Einstein pointed to the failure of overall income to keep pace with potential GDP, itself the result of too low wages (relative to productivity) resulting in what he referred to as technological unemployment.

Drawing on earlier work that examined wealth-generating material processes from the viewpoint of theoretical physics, specifically kinetics, this book provided the theoretical underpinnings of what many at the time, including Irving Fisher, referred to as "acceleration." Drawing extensively from the physical laws that govern material processes (kinetics), it was shown that the technological progress that he and others referred to was inexorably linked to energy use, specifically the introduction throughout the 1920s of electric unit drive–based acceleration, something that the General Electric Company referred to as the "magic of speed."

The model was then used to highlight and corroborate Einstein's predictions as to the implications of this technological shock on output and employment and evaluate his policy prescriptions. As a number of writers have pointed out, the latter were consistent with those contained in the Roosevelt Administration's 1933 signature piece of legislation, the National Industrial Recovery Act, and the National Labor Relations Act of 1936.

That he was unable to grasp, despite his training in physics, just what it was that was driving the spectacular growth in productivity and output can be attributed in large part to the state of economics in the 1920s and

1930s, which he referred to as "muddled."[1] Perhaps a better description would be primitive as it lacked the structure and content of the science of material processes, namely, basic mechanics, thermodynamics, and kinetics. Interestingly, 1921 Nobel laureate in Chemistry-turned-political economist Frederick Soddy would make a similar point, namely, that economics was, from a scientific point of view, fundamentally flawed given its orthogonality to the physics of material processes in general. However, unlike Einstein, he would labor for years to correct this. This would explain, in part, the muddled nature (of economics) Einstein referred to.

One could argue that the book's findings are more Einsteinian than those of Einstein himself in that it draws on the basic physics of material processes specifically on the role of classical mechanics, thermodynamics, and kinetics to explain that which appeared to be beyond his reach in so far as the causes of the Great Depression are concerned. It is ironic that despite his great perspicacity, he was unable to put his finger on the actual underlying cause. Perhaps this owed to the reverence he had for the economics profession, where growth was seen as resulting from labor, capital, and technology. Clearly, had he abandoned this in favor of a physics-based approach where the exact cause had been identified and measured, his writings on the Great Depression would have constituted a major scientific breakthrough, perhaps on a par with the theory of relativity.[2]

As we have shown, he was but one of a whole host of scholars, writers, and observers to view technical progress as the underlying cause of the Great Depression view in the 1920s and 1930s. Others include Rexford

[1] Surprisingly, unlike his 1921 fellow Nobel laureate Frederick Soddy, he stopped short of attempting to make sense of production theory from the point of view of elementary physics. This is all the more surprising as the "technical progress" in question consisted of acceleration and speed, two of the pillars of his theory of relativity (general and special).

[2] Solving the mystery of the Great Depression, it could be argued, would have been of greater value to the world than the theory of relativity.

G. Tugwell, the architect of the New Deal, Howard Scott and the technocracy movement, Irving Fisher, and Clifford Douglas, the father of the social credit doctrine. All pointed to technical progress without providing a convincing, fact-based narrative of just what it was that was increasing productivity.

Had production theory been up to snuff, so to speak, there is every reason to believe that the ideas of Einstein and his like-minded contemporaries would have carried more weight in the then ongoing debate over the causes of the Great Depression. However, by the same token, had production theory resembled that found in Chap. 4, there is every reason to believe that there would not have been a debate to begin with.

In conclusion, the book's main contribution consists of opening the Pandora's box of technological change which myriad writers, scholars, politicians, and laymen both in the 1930s and since have pointed to as the cause of the Great Depression and identifying the key, overriding cause, namely, the electric unit drive–based acceleration of the majority of wealth-creating material processes. The result is a more incisive, more definite, more convincing account of the events of the 1920s and 1930s and a better appreciation of the ideas of scholars like Albert Einstein.

Its other contributions consist of shedding light on the physics of material process acceleration and speed-ups, the main source of productivity growth in the industrial age, and the role of conventional capital and labor. As was argued in Chap. 4, the only possible and actual increase in overall productivity consists of speed-ups. The latter are what fueled the industrial revolutions and all of the industrial age wealth. Another important contribution consists of shedding light on the problem of incomizing potential output—in this case, the increase in output from speed-ups. It is our view that the resulting indeterminacy has been the main impediment to transitioning to higher growth in response to acceleration-based technological change throughout the industrial age.

References

Alexander, B. (1997). Failed cooperation in heterogeneous industries under national recovery administration. *The Journal of Economic History, 57*, 322–344.

Arthmar, R., & Boianovsky, M. (2024). Einstein, Fisher, science and the great depression. *The European Journal of the History of Economic Thought, 31*(6), 948–975.

Babbage, C. (1832). *On the economy of machinery and manufactures*. Charles Knight.

Backman, J. (1962). *The economics of the electrical machinery industry*. New York University Press.

Bakker, G., Crafts, N., & Woltjer, P. (2015). *A vision of the growth process in a technologically progressive economy: The United States, 1929–1941* (p. 10995). CEPR.

Beard, C. (1933). Review of the industrial discipline and the governmental arts. *American Political Science Review, 27*, 833–835.

Beaudreau, B. C. (1995). The impact of electric power on manufacturing productivity: The case of U.S. manufacturing. *Energy Economics, 17*(3), 231–236.

Beaudreau, B. C. (1996). *Mass production, the stock market crash, and the great depression: The macroeconomics of electrification*. Greenwood Press.

Beaudreau, B. C. (1998). *Energy and organization: Growth and distribution Reexamined*. Greenwood Press.

Beaudreau, B. C. (1999). *Energy and the rise and fall of political economy*. Greenwood Press.

B. C. Beaudreau, *Energy, Einstein, and the Great Depression*, https://doi.org/10.1007/978-3-032-26664-4

Beaudreau, B. C. (2001). The origins of creative destruction. In V. Orati & S. B. Dahiya (Eds.), *Economic theory in the light of Schumpeter's scientific heritage*. Spellbound Publications.

Beaudreau, B. C. (2005). *The National Industrial Recovery Redux: Technology and transitions*. iUniverse.

Beaudreau, B. C. (2007). *Underincome: When markets fail to monetize output*. iUnivderse.

Beaudreau, B. C. (2014a). Electrification, tractorization and motorization: Revisiting the Smoot–Hawley Tariff Act. *Journal of Economic Issues, 48*(4), 1–33.

Beaudreau, B. C. (2014b). Discriminating among tariff-based theories of the stock market crash. *Essays in Economic and Business History, 32*(3), 80–99.

Beaudreau, B. C. (2016a). Why did the National Industrial Recovery act fail? *European Review of Economic History, 20*(1), 79–101.

Beaudreau, B. C. (2016b). The petition against the Smoot–Hawley Tariff Act: What 1,028 economists overlooked. *Real World Economics Review, 74*(2), 124–138.

Beaudreau, B. C. (2017a). Economies of speed, KE=1/2mv2 and the productivity slowdown. *Energy, 124*, 100–113.

Beaudreau, B. C. (2017b). Reexamining the origins of the Smoot–Hawley Tariff Act. *Research in Economic History, 33*, 1–22.

Beaudreau, B. C. (2017c). Electrification, the Smoot–Hawley Tariff Act and the decline in investment expenditure in 1931–1932: Testing the excess capacity hypothesis. *International Advances in Economic Research, 23*(3), 295–308.

Beaudreau, B. C. (2018). Electrification, the Smoot–Hawley Tariff Act and the stock market boom and crash; evidence from longitudinal data. *Journal of Economics and Finance, 42*(3), 631–650.

Beaudreau, B. C. (2019). *Why so slow: The role of continued conversion to electric unit drive in delaying the recovery in the 1930s*. Manuscript. Département d'économique, Université Laval.

Beaudreau, B. C. (2020). *The economics of speed: Machine speed as the key factor in productivity*. Springer.

Beaudreau, B. C. (2023). *The great depression, its origins in acceleration and electric unit drive*. World Scientific.

Beaudreau, B. C. (2025). *Economics as science, a critical history of economic thought*. Taylor and Francis Routledge.

Beaudreau, B. C., & Taylor, J. (2018). Why did the Roosevelt administration think cartels, higher wages and shorter workweeks would promote recovery from the great depression? *The Independent Review, 23*(1), 79–101.

Bell, S. (1940). *Productivity, wages and National Income*. Brookings Institution.

Bernanke, B. S. (1986). Employment, hours, and earnings in the depression: An analysis of eight manufacturing industries. *American Economic Review, 76*(1), 82–109.

Bernstein, M. (1987). *The great depression: Delayed recovery and economic change in America, 1929–1939.* Cambridge University Press.

Bix, A. S. (2000). *Inventing ourselves out of jobs? America's debate over technological unemployment, 1929–1981.* Johns Hopkins University Press.

Bleaney, M. (1976). *Underconsumption theories. A history and critical analysis.* International Publishers.

Bohn, F., & Ely, R. T. (1935). *The great change: Work and wealth in the new age.* T. Nelson and Sons.

Bresnahan, T. F., & Trajtenberg, M. (1995). General purpose technologies engines of growth? *Journal of Econometrics, 65*(1), 83–108.

Brookings, R. E. (1932). *The way forward.* The MacMillan Co.

Callahan, C., McDonald, J. A., & O'Brien, A. P. (1994). Who voted for Smoot–Hawley? *The Journal of Economic History, 54*(3), 683–690.

Carver, T. N. (1925). *The present economic revolution in the United States.* Little, Brown and Company.

Chandler, A. D. (1977). *The visible hand: The managerial revolution in American business.* Harvard University Press.

Chase, S. (1934). *The economy of abundance.* The John Day Company.

Clark, R. (1971). *Einstein—The life and times.* The World Publishing Company.

Cohen, A. (1984). Technical change as historical process: The case of the U.S. pulp and paper industry, 1915–1940. *Journal of Economic History, 44*(3), 775–799.

Cohen, M. R. (1933). Review of the industrial discipline and the governmental arts. *Columbia Law Review, 33*(7), 1273–1277.

Cole, H. L., & Ohanian, L. E. (2004a). New deal policies and the persistence of the great depression. *Journal of Political Economy, 112*(3), 779–816.

Cole, H. L., & Ohanian, L. E. (2004b). New deal policies and the persistence of the great depression: A general equilibrium analysis. *Journal of Political Economy, 114*(4), 779–816.

Congressional Record (various volumes). (n.d.). *U.S. congressional record-senate and house of representatives.* U.S. Government Printing Office.

Crocker, F. B. (1901). The electric distribution of power in the workshops. *Journal of the Franklin Institute, 151*(1), 2–9.

Crocker, F. B., Benedikt, V. M., & Ormsbee, A. F. (1895). Electric power in factories and mills. *Transactions of the American Institute of Electrical Engineers., 12*, 298–311.

Cupitt, R. T., & Elliott, E. (1994). Schattschneider revisited: Senate voting on the Smoot–Hawley Tariff Act of 1930. *Economics and Politics, 6*(3), 187–199.

David, P. (1990). The dynamo and the computer: An historical perspective on the modern productivity paradox. *The American Economic Review, 80*(2), 355–361.

David, P. A., & Wright, G. (2003). General purpose technologies and productivity surges: Historical reflections on the future of the ICT revolution. In P. A. David

& M. Thomas (Eds.), *The economic future in historical perspective.* Oxford University Press.

Day, C. (1904). Discussion on the individual operation of machine tools by electric motors. *Journal of the Franklin Institute, 158*(5), 321–358.

Devine, W. D., Jr. (1983). From shafts to wires: Historical perspective on electrification. *The Journal of Economic History, 43*, 347–372.

Devine, W. D., Jr. (1990). Electrified mechanical drive: The historical power distribution revolution. In S. H. Schurr, C. C. Burwell, W. D. Devine Jr., & S. Sonenblum (Eds.), *Electricity in the American Economy: Agent of technological Progress.* Greenwood Press.

Dice, C. A. (1929). *New levels in the stock market.* McGraw-Hill.

Douglas, P. H. (1927). The modern technique of mass production and its relation to wages. *Proceedings of the Academy of Political Science in the City of New York, 12*(3), 17–42.

Eggertsson, G. (2008). Great expectations and the end of the depression. *American Economic Review, 98*(4), 1476–1516.

Eichengreen, B. (1989). The political economy of the Smoot–Hawley tariff. In R. L. Ransom, P. H. Lindert, & R. Sutch (Eds.), *Research in economic history* (Vol. 12, pp. 1–43).

Eichengreen, B. (1992a). *Golden fetters: The gold standard and the great depression, 1919–1929.* Oxford University Press.

Eichengreen, B. (1992b). The origins and nature of the great slump revisited. *The Economic History Review, 45*(2), 213–239.

Eichengreen, B., & O'Rourke, K. H. (2009). A tale of two depressions. *Advisor Perspectives*, April 21. https://citeseerx.ist.psu.edu/viewdoc/download?doi=10.1.1.520.3990&rep=rep1&type=pdf

Einstein, A. (1950). *Out of my later years.* Philosophical Library.

Einstein, A. (1932). The way to a new prosperity! *Nash's Pall Mall, 52-53*, 114–115.

Einstein, A. (1934). *The world as I see it.* Translated by Alan Harris. New York: Covici Friede.

Einstein, A. (1949). Why socialism? *Monthly Review, 1*(1), 9–15. https://ssrn.com/abstract=456824236

Ezekiel, M. (1936). Population and unemployment. *The Annals of the American Academy of Political and Social Science, 188*, 230–242.

Faulkner, H. U. (1950). *From Versailles to the new Deal.* Yale University Press.

Field, A. J. (2003). The most technologically progressive decade of the century. *American Economic Review, 93*(4), 1399–1413.

Field, A. J. (2018). *The impact of world war II on growth of U.S. potential output.* Santa Clara University Working Paper.

Filene, E. A. (1923). The minimum wage and efficiency. *American Economic Review, 13*, 411–415.

Filene, E. A. (1924). *The way out: A forecast of coming changes in American business and industry*. Doubleday, Page and Co.

Filene, E. A. (1929). Mass production makes a better world. *Atlantic Monthly, 143*, 625–631.

Filene, E. A. (1931). *Successful living in this machine age*. Simon and Schuster.

Fisher, I. (1930). *The stock market crash– and after*. The Macmillan Company.

Fisher, I. (1932). *Booms and depressions*. Adelphi.

Fisher, I. (1933). The debt-deflation theory of great depressions. *Econometrica, 1*(4), 37–57.

Fisher, I., & Filene, E. (1936). Do high wages make prosperity? Two points of view on permanent recovery. *Forum, 96*(4), 158–164.

Ford, H. (1922). *My life and work*. Garden City Publishing Co.

Ford, H. (1926a). *Today and tomorrow*. Doubleday.

Ford, H. (1926b). Mass production. *Encyclopaedia Britannica, 13*, 821–823.

Foster, W. T., & Catchings, W. (1927). *Business without a buyer*. Houghton Mifflin.

Friedman, M., & Schwartz, A. J. (1963). *A monetary history of the United States 1867–1960*. National Bureau of Economic Research.

Galbraith, J. K. (1954). *The great crash of 1929*. Houghton Mifflin.

General Electric Company. (1937). *Machine tool speed show*. https://www. youtube.com/watch?v=CUYajEF7X-U&t=344s

Giedion, S. (1948). *Mechanization takes command*. Oxford University Press.

Gordon, R. J. (1961). *Business fluctuations*. Harper & Brothers.

Gordon R. J. (2014). The demise of U.S. economic growth: Restatement, rebuttal, and reflections, NBER working paper 19895, Cambridge.

Gordon, R. J. (2016). *The rise and fall of American growth: The U.S. standard of living since the civil war*. Princeton University Press.

Grytten, O. H. (2008). Why was the great depression not so great in the Nordic countries?: Economic policy and unemployment. *The Journal of European Economic History, 34*, 369–403.

Hansen, A. (1977). *The American economy*. Greenwood Press.

Hawley, E. (1974). Herbert Hoover, the Commerce Secretariat, and the Vision of an "Associative State," 1921–1928. *Journal of American History, 61*(1), 116–140.

Hopkins, W. (1933). Review of the industrial discipline and the governmental arts. *Economic Journal, 33*(9), 500–502.

Hounshell, D. A. (1984). *From the American system to mass production 1800–1932*. The Johns Hopkins University Press.

Hughes, T. P. (1976). Technology and public policy: The failure of giant power. *Proceedings of the IEEE, 64*(9), 1361–1371.

Hughes, T. P. (1983). *Networks of power: Electrification in Western society 1880–1930*. The Johns Hopkins University Press.

Hunter, L., & Bryant, L. (1991). A history of industrial power in the United States 1780–1930 *Volume 3*. In *The transmission of power*. MIT Press.

Irwin, D. A. (2011). *Peddling protectionism: Smoot–Hawley and the great depression*. Princeton University Press.

Irwin, D. A., & Kroszner, R. S. (1996). Log-rolling and economic interests in the passage of the Smoot–Hawley Tariff. *Carneige–Rochester Conference Series on Public Policy, 45*, 173–200.

Isaacson, W. (2007). *Einstein, His Life and Universe*. Simon and Schuster.

Jerome, H. (1934). *Mechanization in industry*. National Bureau of Economic Research.

Jevons, W. S. (1865). *The coal question*. Macmillan and Co.

Jevons, W. S. (1871). *The theory of political economy*. Macmillan and Co.

Kahn, R. F. (1931). The relation of home investment to unemployment. *The Economic Journal, 41*, 173–198.

Keynes, J. M. (1936). *The general theory of employment, output and money*. Palgrave Macmillan.

Kimball, D. (1929). *Changes in new and old industries, in conference on unemployment 1929 report of the committee on recent economic changes of the President's conference on unemployment, Herbert hoover, chairman, including the reports of a special staff of the National Bureau of economic research, Inc. Washington, D.C., committee on recent economic changes*. McGraw-hill.

Klein, M. (2001). The stock market crash of 1929: A review article. *Business History Review, 75*(2), 325–351.

Knight, F. (1921). *Risk, uncertainty and profit*. Houghton Mifflin Co., The Riverside Press.

Kondratieff, N. A. (1926). *The long waves of economic life*. The Institute for Business Cycle Research.

Kondratiev, N. D. (1925). The major economic cycles. In N. Makasheva, W. Samuels, & V. Barnett (Eds.), *The works of Nikolai D. Kondratiev*. Pickering and Chatto.

Kummel, R., Henn, J., & Lindenberger, D. (2002). Capital labor, energy and productivity: Modeling innovation diffusion. *Structural Change and Economic Dynamics, 13*(1), 41–53.

Lacey, R. (1986). *Ford: The men and the machine*. Little Brown and Company.

Laing, G. (1933). *Towards technocracy*. Angelus Press.

Lederer, E. (1925). Konjunktur und Krisen (Business Cycles and Crises). In *Grundriss der Sozialökonomik*. J.C.B. Mohr.

Lederer, E. H. (1938). *Technical Progress and unemployment*. International Labor Office.

Loeb, H. (1935). *The chart of plenty: A study of America's product capacity based on the findings of the National Survey of potential product capacity*. Viking Press.

Lorant, J. H. (1967). Technological change in American manufacturing during the 1920s. *The Journal of Economic History, 27*(2), 243–246.

Lyon, L. S., Homan, P. T., Terborgh, G., Lorwin, L. L., Dearing, C., & Marshall, L. C. (1935). *The National Recovery Administration: An analysis and appraisal.* Brookings Institution.

Marshall, A. (1890). *Principles of economics.* Macmillan.

Marx, K. (1867). *Das Kapital.* Verlag von Otto Meisner.

McGrattan, E., & Prescott, E. (2004). Irving Fisher was right. *International Economic Review, 45*, 991–1009.

Merrill, M. (1990). *Reed Smoot: Apostle in politics.* Utah State University.

Mitchell, B. R. (2003). *International historical statistics: Europe, 1750–2000.* Palgrave Macmillan.

Moulton, H. G. (1935). *Income and economic progress.* The Brookings Institution.

National Bureau of Economic Research. (1929). *Recent economic changes in the United States, volumes 1 and 2.* National Bureau of Economic Research.

National Bureau of Economic Research. (2014). *NBER macrohistory database.* http://www.nber.org/databases/macrohistory/contents/index.html

National Recovery Administration. (1936). *Codes of fair competition* (Vol. 6, pp. 245–286). United States Government Printing Office.

Neiser, H. (1934). General overproduction: A study of Say's law of markets. *Journal of Political Economy, 42*(4), 433–465.

Neisser, H. (1936). *Some international aspects of the business cycle.* University of Pennsylvania Press.

Nevins, A. (1954). *Ford: The times, the man, the company.* Charles Scribner's Sons.

New York Times (various editions). (n.d.). *New York Times. New York Times.*

Nourse, E. G., Tryon, F. G., Drury, H. B., Leven, M., Moulton, H. G., & Lewis, C. (1934). *America's capacity to produce.* Brookings Institution.

Nye, D. E. (1990). *Electrifying America: Social meanings of a new technology.* MIT Press.

Oshima, H. T. (1984). The growth of U.S. factor productivity: The significance of new technologies in the early decades of the twentieth century. *Journal of Economic History, 44*(1), 161–170.

Pastor, R. (1980). *Congress and the politics of United States foreign economic policy, 1929–1976.* University of California Press.

Pecora, F. (1939). *Wall street under oath: The story of our modern money changers.* A.M. Kelley.

Polakov, W. N. (1933). *The power age, its quest and challenge.* Covici, Friede Publishers.

Porter, H. A. (1932). *Roosevelt and Technocracy.* Wetzel Publishing Company.

Powell, J. (2003). *FDR's folly: How Roosevelt and his new Deal prolonged the great depression.* Three Rivers Press.

Ramey, V. (2011). Can government purchases stimulate the economy? *Journal of Economic Literature, 49*(3), 673–685.

Robinson, J. (1937). *Essays in the theory of employment.* Macmillan.

Rodbertus, J. K. (1850). *Sociale Briefe an von Kirchmann.* (Social Letters to von Kirchmann). Gerhard.

Romasco, A. U. (1983). *The politics of recovery.* Oxford University Press.

Rosenberg, N. (1972). *Technology and American economic growth.* M.E. Sharpe.

Rosenberg, N., & Birdzell, L. E., Jr. (1986). *How the west grew rich: The transformation of the industrial world.* Basic Books.

Rowe, D. E., & Schulmann, R. (Eds.). (2009). *Einstein on politics: His private thoughts and public stands on nationalism, Zionism, war, peace, and the bomb.* Princeton University Press.

Schattschneider, E. E. (1935). *Politics, pressures, and the tariff.* Prentice Hall.

Schumpeter, J. A. (1928). The instability of capitalism. *The Economic Journal, 38*(151), 361–386.

Schurr, S. H., Burwell, C. C., Devine, W. D., Jr., & Sonenblum, S. (Eds.). (1990). *Electricity in the American Economy: Agent of technological Progress.* Greenwood Press.

Scott, H., et al. (1933). *Introduction to technocracy.* The John Day Company.

Shiller, R. J. (2000). *Irrational exuberance.* Princeton University Press.

Simonde de Sismondi, J. C. L. (1819). *Nouveaux Principes d'Économie Politique.* Delaunay.

Sirkin, G. (1975). The stock market of 1929 revisited: A note. *Business History Review, 44*(3), 223–231.

Smith, A. (1976). *An inquiry into the nature and causes of the wealth of nations, 1776.* W. Strahan and T. Cadell.

Soddy, F. (1922). *Cartesian economics: The bearing of physical science upon state stewardship.* Hendersons.

Sonenblum, S. (1990). Electrification and productivity growth in manufacturing. In S. H. Schurr, C. C. Burwell, W. D. Devine Jr., & S. Sonenblum (Eds.), *Electricity in the American Economy: Agent of technological Progress.* Greenwood Press.

Soule, G. (1947). *Prosperity decade: From war to depression 1917–1929.* Rinehart and Company.

Steindl, F. G. (2004). *Understanding economic recovery in the 1930s: Endogenous propagation in the great depression.* University of Michigan Press.

Stresing, R., Lindenberger, D., & Kummel, R. (2008). Cointegration of output, capital, labor and energy. *The European Physical Journal B: Condensed Matter and Complex Systems, 66*(2), 279–287.

Szostak, R. (1996). *Technological innovation and the great depression.* Routledge, Taylor and Francis.

Tapley, W. H. (1899). The practical application of electric motors to printing press machinery. *Journal of the Franklin Institute, 148*(4), 259–279.

Taussig, F. (1930). The tariff, 1929–1930. *The Quarterly Journal of Economics, 44*(2), 175–204.

Taylor, J. E. (2011). Work-sharing during the great depression: Did the presidents reemployment agreement promote reemployment? *Economica, 78*, 133–158.

Taylor, J. E. (2019). *Deconstructing the monolith: The microeconomics of the National Industrial Recovery act.* University of Chicago Press.

Taylor, J. E., & Klein, P. G. (2008). An anatomy of a cartel: The national industrial recovery act of 1933 and the compliance crisis of 1934. *Research in Economic History, 26*, 235–271.

Taylor, J. E., Neumann, T., & Fishback, P. (2013). Comparisons of weekly hours over the past century and the importance of work sharing policies in the 1930s. *American Economic Review Papers and Proceedings, 103*(3), 105–110.

Taylor, J. E., & Neumann, T. C. (2016). Recovery spring, faltering fall: March to November 1933. *Explorations in Economic History, 61*(3), 54–67.

Thomas, W. (1928). The economic significance of the increased efficiency of American industry. *American Economic Review, 18*(1), 122–138.

Tryon, F. G. (1927). An index of consumption of fuels and water power. *Journal of the American Statistical Association, 22*(2), 271–282.

Tugwell, R. G. (1927). *Industry's coming of age.* Columbia University Press.

Tugwell, R. G. (1933). *The industrial arts and the governmental arts.* Columbia University Press.

U.S. Bureau of Census. (1914). *Abstract of the census of the manufactures1909.* Government Printing Office.

U.S. Bureau of the Census. (1923). *Abstract of the census of manufactures 1919.* Government Printing Office.

U.S. Bureau of the Census. (1949). *Historical statistics of the United States 1789–1945.* Government Printing Office.

U.S. Committee of Industrial Analysis. (1937). *The national recovery administration: Report of the President's committee of industrial analysis.* Department of Commerce.

U.S. Department of Commerce. (1975). *Historical statistics of the United States, colonial times to 1970.* U.S. Government Printing Office.

U.S. Department of Labor. (1966). Technical trends in major North American industries. Department of Labor Statistics No. 1474, Washington, DC.

Veblen, T. (1921). *The engineers and the Price system.* Huebsch.

Vedder, R. K., & Galloway, L. E. (1993). *Out of work: Unemployment and government in twentieth century America.* Holmes and Meier.

Woirol, G. (2006). New data, new issues: The origins of the technological unemployment debates. *History of Political Economy, 38*(3), 473–496.

Wright, G. (1990). The origins of American industrial success, 1879–1940. *American Economic Review, American Economic Association, 80*(4), 651–668.

Index[1]

[1] Note: Page numbers followed by 'n' refer to notes.

B. C. Beaudreau, *Energy, Einstein, and the Great Depression*, https://doi.org/10.1007/978-3-032-26664-4

FSC
www.fsc.org
MIX
Papier | Fördert
gute Waldnutzung
FSC® C083411

Kolibri 360 GmbH
Ferdinand-Jühlke-Straße 7
99095 Erfurt, Deutschland
produktsicherheit@kolibri360.de